THE MAN OF LAWLESSNESS

The Antichrist in the Tribulation

THE MAN OF LAWLESSNESS

The Antichrist in the Tribulation

". . . the day of the Lord . . . will not come unless the apostasy comes first, and the man of lawlessness is revealed, the son of destruction, who opposes and exalts himself above every so-called god or object of worship, so that he takes his seat in the temple of God, displaying himself as being God."

— 2 Thessalonians 2:2b-4

". . . there will be a great tribulation, such as has not occurred since the beginning of the world until now, nor ever will."

— Matthew 24:21

Dr. David R. Reagan

LAMB & LION MINISTRIES
McKinney, Texas

Dedicated to

My daughters, Ruth Reagan and Rachel Houck,
and
to Rachel's husband, Leo.

In appreciation for their encouragement over many years.

First edition, 2012

ISBN: 978-0-945593-20-1

Library of Congress Control Number: 2012903806

Lamb & Lion Ministries
P.O. Box 919
McKinney, Texas 75070
lamblion@lamblion.com
www.lamblion.com

Cover design by Trey Collich,
Media Minister for Lamb & Lion Ministries.

Printed in the United States of America.

CONTENTS

Part 4:
Good News for Christians

Part 5:
Are You Ready?

> "The whole time of your faith will not profit you unless you are made complete in the last time. For in the last days false prophets and corrupters shall be multiplied, and sheep shall be turned into wolves . . . and then shall the deceiver of the world appear, pretending to be the Son of God, and [he] shall do signs and wonders, and the earth shall be delivered into his hands" (Didache 16:3-4).

The Didache (meaning "Teaching")is a brief early Christian treatise, dated by most scholars to the late First Century, around 80 AD. Its full title is "Teaching of the Lord to the Gentiles (or Nations) by the Twelve Apostles." It is referenced in the writings of Eusebius who lived from 260 to 341 AD. The document was lost for centuries. It was rediscovered by a Greek Orthodox priest in 1873 and published in English for the first time in 1883.

> "We do not want another committee, we have too many already. What we want is a man of sufficient stature to hold the allegiance of all the people and to lift us up out of the economic morass into which we are sinking. Send us such a man, and whether he be God or devil, we will receive him." — Paul Henri Spaak (1899-1972).

Paul Henri Spaak served as the first president of the United Nations General Assembly (1946-1947). He also served as prime minister of Belgium several times (1938-1939, 1946, 1947-1949) and was one of the early planners of the European Common Market. His final international leadership position was Secretary General of NATO (1957-1961).

Books by Dr. David R. Reagan

(Most of these have been published in foreign languages.)

The Christ in Prophecy Study Guide (McKinney, TX: Lamb & Lion Ministries, 1987). Second edition in 2001.

Trusting God: Learning to Walk by Faith (Lafayette, LA: Huntington House, 1987). Second edition in 1994.

Jesus is Coming Again! (Eugene, OR: Harvest House, 1992).

The Master Plan: Making Sense of the Controversies Surrounding Bible Prophecy Today (Eugene, OR: Harvest House, 1993).

Living for Christ in the End Times (Green Forest, AR: New Leaf Press, 2000).

Wrath and Glory: Unveiling the Majestic Book of Revelation (Green Forest, AR: New Leaf Press, 2001).

America the Beautiful? The United States in Bible Prophecy (McKinney, TX: Lamb & Lion Ministries, 2003). Second edition in 2006. Third edition in 2009.

God's Plan for the Ages: The Blueprint of Bible Prophecy (McKinney, TX: Lamb & Lion Ministries, 2005).

Eternity: Heaven or Hell? (McKinney, TX: Lamb & Lion Ministries, 2010).

Jesus: The Lamb and The Lion (McKinney, TX: Lamb & Lion Ministries, 2011).

PREFACE

For years I have taught that when studying or teaching Bible prophecy, the focus of attention should be on Jesus Christ and not on the Antichrist. Accordingly, I have produced several books that explore in detail what Bible prophecy has to say about the Messiah, and I have attempted to show how those prophecies were literally fulfilled in the life of Jesus.

I never expected to write a book about the Antichrist. But I felt compelled to do so when I began to notice a steady stream of books and articles being published about the Antichrist, most of which were very sensational in nature, and thus serving to divert attention away from Jesus Christ.

This book is an attempt to bring some balance to the subject. The Antichrist is a major topic of end time Bible prophecy, and as such, should not be ignored. But on the other hand, this nefarious character should not be an obsession. We must always keep in mind the words of Revelation 19:10 which say, ". . . the testimony of Jesus is the spirit of prophecy."

The signs of the times clearly indicate that we are on the threshold of what is going to be the most terrible time in all of human history — a time of absolutely unparalleled horror, a time called the Tribulation. During this time a monster referred to in the Scriptures as 'the man of lawlessness" will be responsible for killing one-half of humanity during the first half of the Tribulation. And during the second half, he will murder two-thirds of the Jewish people.

But there is good news in the midst of all this carnage, for the message of the Bible is that we who are believers are going to win in the end. The Tribulation will be cut short at the end of seven years with the triumphant return of Jesus. He will destroy the Antichrist and will replace him as the ruler of this world, bringing peace, righteousness and justice.

And that's not all the good news. The Bible teaches that believers are going to be taken out of this world before the Tribulation begins. Christians will not have to face the Antichrist and his horrors.

In this book, we are going to take a look at a lot of questions that people ask about the end times:

- Why is there going to be a Great Tribulation?
- What are the truths and misconceptions about the Tribulation?
- Why would a God of love allow such devastation?
- Where will the Antichrist come from?
- What will the Antichrist be like?
- Will the Antichrist be a Jew?
- Is it possible that the Antichrist could be a Muslim?
- Where will the Antichrist establish his headquarters?
- Will the Jews accept the Antichrist as their Messiah?
- Will the Antichrist be killed and resurrected from the dead?
- What will be the ultimate destiny of the Antichrist?
- Is the Antichrist alive today, and if so, can he be identified?
- Is the Church really promised an escape from the Great Tribulation, and if so, when?

These and many other questions will be addressed in this book. I will personally respond to each question, but one of the unique aspects of this book is that I have invited 22 Bible prophecy experts to share their opinions about several of these questions. I think you will find their responses to be fascinating and illuminating.

I want to take this opportunity to thank the trustees and staff of Lamb & Lion Ministries for their constant encouragement. I am also very grateful to the Prophecy Partners of our ministry who serve as our prayer warriors and who supply the financial foundation that makes it possible for us to reach so many people with the message of the Lord's soon return.

I also want to express appreciation to the 22 Bible prophecy experts who responded to my questions about the Antichrist. They were very kind to do so, and they were gracious to allow me to quote their responses. I am also grateful to Kay Bien and Jana Olivieri for proof-reading the book.

Most of all I am thankful to the Lord for calling me to serve Him in these end times. When speaking in public forums, I am always delighted to tell people that I am neither a Democrat or a Republican. I am, instead, a Monarchist, because I have devoted my life to doing everything I can to help prepare the way for the return of the King of kings and Lord of lords who will reign in glory and majesty from Mount Zion in Jerusalem and whose reign will bring peace, righteousness and justice to all the world.

Maranatha!

Dr. David R. Reagan
Allen, Texas
Spring 2012

"By means of the events which shall occur in the time of the Antichrist it is shown that he, being an apostate and a robber, is anxious to be adored as God, and that although a mere slave, he wishes to be proclaimed as king. For he, being endued with all the power of the devil, shall not come as a righteous king nor as a legitimate king in subjection to God, but as an impious, unjust, and lawless one . . . setting aside idols to persuade [men] that he himself is God, raising himself up as the only idol . . ."

— Irenaeus, *Against Heresies* 5:25:1-2

Irenaeus (2nd century AD – c. 202) was Bishop of Lugdunum in Gaul, then a part of the Roman Empire (now Lyon, France). He was an early church father and apologist, and his writings were formative in the early development of Christian theology. In his youth, he was taught the fundamentals of the Christian faith by Polycarp of Smyrna, who, in turn, was a disciple of the Apostle John. Irenaeus' best-known book, *Against Heresies* (c. 180) is a detailed attack on Gnosticism.

PART 1
THE ANTICHRIST IN SCRIPTURE

". . . there will be a great tribulation, such as has not occurred since the beginning of the world until now, nor ever will. Unless those days had been cut short, no life would have been saved; but for the sake of the elect those days will be cut short." — Jesus, Matthew 24:21-22

A TIME OF UNPARALLELED HORROR

"Now at that time Michael, the great prince who stands guard over the sons of your people, will arise. And there will be a time of distress such as never occurred since there was a nation until that time; and at that time your people, everyone who is found written in the book, will be rescued." — Daniel 12:1

I receive several phone calls each year from people — some of them ministers — asking me if I think we are in the Tribulation yet. I always respond by telling them that when the Tribulation begins, the people who are on earth will not have to call anyone to find out for sure whether or not it has begun. The Tribulation will be a living hell with a degree of violence that is unparalleled in all of history.

The Bible gives us a lot of information about this horrible period of seven years that is fast approaching. The entire book of Zephaniah is devoted to it. In addition, many other Old Testament passages, like Isaiah 24, provide descriptions of it. And a total of fourteen chapters in the book of Revelation focus on it (Revelation 6-19).

But despite all this information, there are many myths concerning the Great Tribulation that circulate among Christians. For example, many argue that the first half of this time period will be peaceful and that only the second half will be characterized by intense warfare. Other misconceptions relate to the Antichrist and the Church.

The Concept

Before we consider some of these myths and misconceptions, let's familiarize ourselves more thoroughly with the concept of the Tribulation.

The first mention of the Tribulation in the Bible is found in Deuteronomy 4:27-30. Before the Children of Israel entered the Promised Land, Moses warned them that if they were unfaithful to God, they would be scattered among the nations. He then prophesied that "in the latter days" they would come under "distress," and the result would be their "return to the Lord."

Centuries later, Jeremiah used the same terminology when he referred to the Tribulation. He called it "the time of Jacob's distress" (Jeremiah 30:7). In like manner, Daniel called it "a time of distress," and he prophesied it would be the worst period of trouble in the history of the Jewish people (Daniel 12:1). Malachi stated it would be a time of refining for the Jews, as when silver is purified by fire (Malachi 3:1-4). And Zechariah used the same imagery when he prophesied that two-thirds of the Jewish people will perish during this time. Of the remnant remaining, he wrote, "I [the Lord] will bring the third part through the fire [and] refine them as silver is refined . . ." (Zechariah 13:8-9).

The Scope

The Jews will not be the only ones to suffer during this period of unparalleled trouble. The Bible makes it clear that all the nations of the world will experience catastrophic calamities.

Isaiah says it will be "a day of reckoning" for all the nations of the world (Isaiah 2:10-17). Zephaniah says that "all the earth will be devoured in the fire of God's jealousy" (Zephaniah 1:18). Here's how the psalmist Asaph put it: "A cup is in the hand of the Lord, and the wine foams . . . surely, all the wicked of the earth must drain and drink down its dregs" (Psalm 75:8).

The Length

The prophet Daniel defined the length of the Tribulation. He said God would accomplish all His purposes for the Jewish people during a period of 70 weeks of years (490 years). Sixty-nine of those weeks of years (483 years) would lead up to the death of the Messiah. The final week of years would occur at the end of the age, right before the return of the Messiah (Daniel 9:24-27). This concluding week of years (7 years) corresponds to the Tribulation for, as Daniel put it, it will mark the time when "the prince who is to come" will "make desolate" — a reference to the Antichrist.

The timing established by Daniel is confirmed in the book of Revelation where the Tribulation is divided into two periods of 3½ years each (Revelation 11:3,7 and 13:5). The dividing point between the two halves of the Tribulation will occur when the Antichrist reveals himself by entering the rebuilt Temple in Jerusalem, stopping the sacrifices, and declaring himself to be God (Matthew 24:15, 2 Thessalonians 2:3-4, and Revelation 13:5-6).

The Starting Point

When will this terrible period begin? The Bible says in general terms that it will start after the Jews have been regathered and have been re-established in their homeland and in their sacred city of Jerusalem.

Specifically, the Bible says it will begin at a time when all the world comes together against Israel over the issue of who will control the city of Jerusalem (Zechariah 12:2-3). In short, we are on the very threshold of the Tribulation today as we witness the United Nations, the European Union, the Vatican, and the Arab nations demanding that the Jews surrender their sovereignty over Jerusalem.

The specific event that will mark the seven year countdown of the Tribulation will be the signing of a peace treaty negotiated between Israel and her Arab enemies by the Antichrist — a treaty that will allow the Jews to rebuild their Temple (Daniel 9:27).

The Nature

The unparalleled horror of the Tribulation is spelled out in detail in both the Hebrew Scriptures and the New Testament. Isaiah wrote that it will be a day of "the terror of the Lord" when "the pride of men will be abased" (Isaiah 2:10,17,19). Zephaniah proclaimed that it will be a "day of wrath," "a day of trouble and distress," and "a day of destruction and desolation" (Zephaniah 1:15). Men will stumble around like they are blind and "their blood will be poured out like dust" (Zephaniah 1:17).

This dreary picture is echoed in the New Testament. Jesus said it will be a time of tribulation "such as has not occurred since the beginning of the world until now, nor ever shall" (Matthew 24:21). In fact, Jesus said it will be so terrible that if it were not stopped at the end of seven years, it would result in the destruction of all life (Matthew 24:22). The Apostle John states that the chaos will be so great that the leaders of the world will crawl into caves and cry out for the rocks of the mountains to fall upon them (Revelation 6:15-16).

Misconceptions

With this biblical background, let's turn our attention now to some of the misconceptions that exist regarding the Tribulation. Five of the major ones that I would identify are listed below:

1) The Antichrist will rise to world power through cunning, flattery, and deception.

2) The whole world will flock to the Antichrist in awe

and adoration.

3) The Jews will accept the Antichrist as their Messiah.

4) There will be 3½ years of peace followed by 3½ years of war.

5) The Antichrist will be the most brilliant and effective leader in world history.

The Antichrist's Rise to Power

The idea that the Antichrist will rise to world power through shrewdness and skilled diplomacy is based on Daniel 8:23-25a. These verses say a king will arise who is "skilled in intrigue" and who "will succeed through the practice of deceit."

But the same passage also says that he "will destroy to an extraordinary degree." He will destroy both "mighty men and the people of the saints." Many of these he will destroy "while they are at peace" (Daniel 8:24-25a).

These verses make it very clear that the Antichrist is going to use both diplomacy and military power to gain control of the world. The likeliest scenario is that he will initially rise to power in Europe through the use of shrewd diplomacy. But he will extend his power from his European base through war.

The World's "Acceptance" of the Antichrist

I believe his conquering of the world through the use of military power is what is pictured in Revelation 6:1-8. This passage pictures the Antichrist going forth at the beginning of the Tribulation with a bow "to conquer." A red horse representing war "takes peace from the earth." The result is widespread suffering and the death of one-fourth of humanity by the sword, famine, pestilence, and wild beasts.

It is a misconception to believe the non-European world will flock to the Antichrist in awe and adoration. The world outside of Europe is not going to submit willingly to the control of the Antichrist, no matter how charismatic and dynamic he may be.

Keep in mind that the nations of Asia, Africa, and Latin America have fought for the past 100 years to rid themselves of European colonial rule. They are not going to passively submit themselves to a renewal of that rule. They will fight, and the result — as Revelation 6 so clearly indicates — will be a horrible world war of unprecedented magnitude.

Acceptance of the Antichrist by the Jews

The idea that the Jews will accept the Antichrist as their Messiah during the Tribulation is based upon a statement by Jesus that is recorded in John 5:43. Jesus said, "I have come in my Father's name, and you do not receive Me; if another shall come in his own name, you will receive him."

But the relevant end time passages in Daniel and Revelation seem to make it clear that the acceptance of the Antichrist by the Jews will be as a political redeemer who miraculously works out a peace settlement that will guarantee their safety and will enable them to rebuild their Temple.

There is no indication that they ever accept the Antichrist as a spiritual redeemer — as their Messiah. In fact, when the Antichrist enters the Temple in the middle of the Tribulation and declares himself to be God, the Jews revolt against him (Revelation 12:13-17).

When the revolt occurs, the Antichrist becomes obsessed with annihilating the Jewish people. That is when the "great tribulation" spoken of by Jesus in Matthew 24 will begin.

The Tribulation Holocaust that will occur during the last 3½ years of that terrible period will be far worse than the

Nazi Holocaust. Two-thirds of the Jews will be killed (Zechariah 13:8-9). The Antichrist will be possessed by Satan (Daniel 8:24), and Satan is determined to annihilate the Jews.

Satan's obsession with the Jews stems from the fact that he hates them with a passion. He hates them because they gave the world the Bible. He hates them because the Messiah came through them. He hates them because God loves them, and because God chose them to be a witness of what it means to have a relationship with Him. And Satan hates the Jews because God has promised over and over in His Word that at the end of the Tribulation, He is going to bring a great remnant to salvation through faith in their Messiah, Yeshua (Romans 9-11).

The First Half of the Tribulation

Another misconception relates to the nature of the first half of the Tribulation. Many believe that this period of 3½ years is going to be a time of peace that will be followed by 3½ years of war. Some feel so strongly about this that they use the word, Tribulation, to apply only to the second half of the seven year period.

This view is based primarily on a statement Jesus made that is recorded in Matthew 24. According to this passage, Jesus referred to the last half of Daniel's 70th week of years as "the great tribulation" (Matthew 24:21). But it must be kept in mind that these words of Jesus were directed specifically to the Jewish people.

The second half of the Tribulation will truly be the "time of great tribulation" for the Jews. That's because they will live in peace during the first half of the Tribulation under a covenant guaranteed by the Antichrist. During that time, the Antichrist will be focused on conquering the world. Once he has accomplished that goal — as he will (Revelation 13:7-8) — he will go to Jerusalem, enter the Temple, stop the sacrifices, and desecrate the Temple by erecting a statue of himself (2 Thessalonians 2:3-4).

The Jewish people will be outraged and will respond in a revolt. When they do this, the Antichrist will become obsessed with destroying them. That will be his primary goal during the second half of the Tribulation.

So, to summarize, the Jews will live in peace during the first half of the Tribulation, but not the Gentile nations of the world. The wars of the Antichrist will devastate the world. One-forth of humanity will die in the initial war (Revelation 6:8). That's 1.5 billion people in today's terms. According to Revelation 8 and 9, when the war resumes, one-third of those left alive will die (another 1.5 billion).

The first half of the Tribulation is going to be anything but a time of peace. It will, instead, be a time of unimaginable carnage, for one-half of humanity will die in the first 3½ years!

The Quality of the Antichrist's Leadership

The erroneous concept that the Antichrist will be the world's most brilliant and glorious leader is based on Revelation 13:7 where it says he will gain authority over "every tribe, people, tongue and nation" on planet earth — something no other person has ever done.

But the evidence of prophecy points to the fact that his reign will be anything but brilliant and glorious.

For example, his conquest of the world will devastate the earth. It will be like Napoleon's "victory" in Russia — he will win the battle and lose the war. The Antichrist will end up with a world that is devastated and polluted beyond imagination. Furthermore, the world's subservience to him and worship of him will be based to a large degree on force, deception, and terror — not just genuine admiration.

Also, his obsession with the Jews will undermine his kingdom and ultimately lead to its destruction. Daniel 11:40-45 indicates that when his attention is diverted to the destruction of the Jews, a worldwide revolt will break out against his kingdom. Nations will send armies against him from the North, East and South.

The Antichrist may prove to be a successful military conqueror, but he will be a miserable leader whose world-wide empire will last only 3½ years — and during that time, it will be constantly ravaged by internal revolt.

A Misconception Concerning the Church

Another popular misconception about the Tribulation is that the Church will go through it and suffer mightily at the hands of the Antichrist. This concept is based upon verses like Revelation 13:7 which says that the Antichrist will "make war with the saints."

But I believe the saints referred to here are those who are saved during the Tribulation. There is going to be a great harvest of souls during the Tribulation. Some will be saved in response to the Rapture. Others will respond to the preaching of the Two Witnesses in Jerusalem (Revelation 11). The response of others will be stimulated by the Tribulation judgments which will motivate many to repent. Still others will respond to the special angel who will be sent by God near the end of the Tribulation to proclaim the Gospel to every living creature (Revelation 14:6-7). Many will be saved, but most of these will be martyred for their faith (Revelation 7:9-17).

There is no purpose for the Church during the Tribulation. This will be a time of God's judgment upon the unbelieving Gentiles and Jews who have rejected God's grace, love and mercy expressed in Jesus.

Some argue that the Church must go through the Tribulation to be purged or cleansed. But the true Church has already been purified by the blood of Jesus (Ephesians 5:25-27, 1 John 1:7, and Romans 8:1). The Tribulation is not a Protestant purgatory.

The symbolic imagery of the New Testament focuses on the Church as being the Bride of Christ. Is the Bridegroom going to beat up His Bride for seven years before He comes for her? I think not. The Bible says that Jesus is coming to deliver His Bride from the wrath that is to come (1 Thessalonians 1:10). Also, Revelation 19:8,14 pictures Jesus returning with His Church at the end of the Tribulation, indicating the Redeemed will be taken out of this world before the Tribulation begins.

Revelation focuses on the Church in its first three chapters. Beginning with chapter 4, there is no more mention of the Church during the entire period of the Tribulation. The Church is not referred to again until Revelation 22:16.

The Purpose

What's it all about? Why is there going to be such carnage? How could a God of grace, mercy and love allow such an outbreak of unbridled terror and bloodshed?

One reason is to satisfy the justice of God. Yes, God is characterized by grace, mercy and love, but He is also a God of perfect justice, righteousness and holiness. Therefore, He must deal with sin. His justice demands it. Even His love compels it. How could a God of true love simply overlook the actions of a murderer or a pedophile?

The prophet Nahum understood the true nature of God. He wrote that "The Lord is good, a stronghold in the day of trouble, and He knows those who take refuge in Him" (Nahum 1:7). That is the love and mercy of God. But the same prophet also wrote (Nahum 1:2-3):

> A jealous and avenging God is the Lord;
> The Lord is avenging and wrathful.
> The Lord takes vengeance on His adversaries,
> And He reserves wrath for His enemies.
> The Lord is slow to anger and great in power,
> And the Lord will by no means leave the
> guilty unpunished.

Truly, the Lord is "slow to anger." He allows the iniquities of Mankind to accumulate over long periods of time because He does not wish that any should perish (2 Peter 3:9). His desire, instead, is that all should come to repentance. But there is always a day of reckoning, just as there was in the days of Noah, and such a day has been set for this age. Paul referred to it in his sermon in Athens when he said, "He [God] has fixed a day in which He will judge the world in righteousness" (Acts 17:31).

A second reason for the Tribulation is to bring people to salvation. Amazingly, even when God pours out His wrath, His fundamental purpose is not to destroy but to save. Isaiah 26:9 explains it this way: "When the earth experiences Your judgments, the inhabitants of the world learn righteousness."

The brutal fact is that God often has to hit us over the head with a two-by-four in order to get our attention and motivate us to repentance. The equally brutal fact is that most people respond to such discipline by either cursing God or continuing to ignore Him (Revelation 9:20-21). But some people always respond in humility and are saved. As Billy Graham has put it: "The same sun that melts the butter, hardens the clay."

When God's wrath is poured out during the Tribulation, some hearts will be melted, but most will be hardened, illustrating once again that nothing is as "deceitful" and "desperately sick" as the heart of Man (Jeremiah 17:9).

Conclusion

Man is frivolous about sin. God is serious. The Tribulation will be a graphic expression of how serious God is about Mankind's rebellion against Him.

The signs of the times are shouting that we are standing on the threshold of the Tribulation. The message of the Holy Spirit is "Come out of Babylon" (Revelation 18:4). That message means for us to separate ourselves from the love of this world and prepare ourselves for eternity. For believers, it means a commitment to holiness. For unbelievers it means a commitment to Jesus as Lord and Savior before He returns as God's avenger.

The time remaining is short. The time for action is now.

A TYRANT OF UNBRIDLED RUTHLESSNESS

"[Gabriel] said to me [Daniel], 'Behold, I am going to let you know what will occur at the final period of the indignation, for it pertains to the appointed time of the end . . . A king will arise, insolent and skilled in intrigue. His power will be mighty . . . and he will destroy to an extraordinary degree . . ."

— Daniel 8:19, 23b-24a

The Bible teaches that in the end times, right before the return of Jesus, the greatest political leader in the history of Mankind will emerge from Europe. After taking over that area by diplomatic cunning and deceit, he will launch a military campaign that will result in his acquiring "authority over every tribe and people and tongue and nation" (Revelation 13:7). His empire will be the most extensive in all of history, encompassing the entire world, and his rule will be the most demonic the world has ever experienced.

He will begin his rise to power as a dynamic, charismatic, insightful, visionary leader who will astound the world with the cleverness of his solutions to world problems. He will appear to be the savior of the world. But as he consolidates his power, his true nature will be revealed. He will emerge as a Satan-possessed and empowered person who hates God and is determined to annihilate both Christianity and Judaism. For this reason, he is identified in scripture as the Antichrist (1 John 2:18), for he will stand against God and His anointed one, Jesus Christ.

His Origin

Where will this sinister person come from? Some have speculated that he will come out of Syria since one of his prophetic types in history — Antiochus Epiphanes (215 - 164 BC) — was a Syrian tyrant. But Antiochus was actually of Greek heritage. Could he therefore be a Greek? It is not likely.

It is much more likely that he will rise out of the heartland of the old Roman Empire and that he will be of Italian descent. This conclusion is based upon a statement in Daniel 9:26. In that passage the Antichrist is referred to as "the prince who is to come," and he is identified as being from the people who "will destroy the city and the sanctuary."

We know from history that both Jerusalem and the Jewish Temple were destroyed by the Romans in 70 AD. Therefore, according to Daniel, the Antichrist must be of Roman heritage.

His Ethnic Heritage

Will he be a Jew? Many assume he will be because Jesus said, "I have come in My Father's name, and you do not receive Me; if another shall come in his own name, you will receive him" (John 5:43). Based on this statement, people ask, "How could the Jews possibly receive a Gentile as their Messiah?"

But the Bible does not teach that the Jews will receive the Antichrist as their Messiah. It teaches they will accept him as a great political leader and diplomat and that they will put their trust in him as the guarantor of peace in the Middle East.

But the moment he reveals himself as the Antichrist by desecrating the Jew's rebuilt Temple and blaspheming God, the Jewish people will revolt. They will reject him as Messiah, and he will respond in fury by attempting to annihilate them.

The Antichrist does not have to be a Jew. And, in fact, the Bible makes it clear that he will be a Gentile. In Revelation 13:1 he is portrayed as a "beast coming up out of the sea." The sea is used consistently throughout the prophetic scriptures as a symbol of the Gentile nations (Daniel 7:3; Luke 21:25; and Revelation 17:1).

By contrast, the Antichrist's right hand man, the False Prophet, who will serve as his religious leader, will be a Jew. This is revealed in Revelation 13:11 where it says that John saw "another beast coming up out of the earth [literally, the land]." Just as the sea is used symbolically in prophecy to refer to the Gentile nations, the land (or earth) is used to refer to Israel. This does not mean the False Prophet will be an Orthodox Jew. It only means that he will be of Jewish heritage. Religiously, he will be an apostate Jew who will head up the One World Religion of the Antichrist.

Will He be Killed and Resurrected?

There is one other issue concerning the origin of the Antichrist that we need to consider. Many argue that he will be a person resurrected from the dead — most likely Nero or Judas Iscariot. This assumption is based on a statement in Revelation 13:1-3 where John describes the Antichrist as a beast with seven heads. He then makes the observation that one of his heads appeared "as if it had been slain, and his fatal wound was healed." He comments that "the whole earth was amazed" by this and therefore "followed after the beast" (Revelation 13:3).

The problem with this interpretation is that "the fatal wound" referred to in the passage has nothing to do with the person of the Antichrist. The seven heads represent seven Gentile empires — namely, Egypt, Assyria, Babylon, Medo-Persia, Greece, Rome, and the final empire of the Antichrist.

The head with the fatal wound that has been healed is the Roman Empire. We know this from the book of Daniel where it is prophesied that the Roman Empire will be the last of the Gentile empires until the end times when the empire of the Antichrist will emerge from a reunited Europe — that is, from a revival of the old Roman Empire (Daniel 2:31-45 and 7:1-8, 24-28).

The prophecies of Daniel have proved to be absolutely accurate. The Roman Empire was the last of the Gentile empires. It disintegrated into the nation-state system that has prevailed to this day. There have been numerous military attempts to resurrect the Roman Empire, most notably by Napoleon and Hitler. Today, the core of the empire is coalescing before our eyes through diplomatic means, producing a united Europe that will serve as the base for the rise of the Antichrist.

Another passage that is used to justify the idea of the Antichrist being a resurrected person is Zechariah 11:17 —

> Woe to the worthless shepherd
> Who leaves the flock!
> A sword will be on his arm
> And on his right eye!
> His arm will be totally withered,
> And his right eye will be blind.

It is argued that this passage indicates that the Antichrist will be a person who has suffered a fatal wound. Now, there is no doubt this passage refers to the Antichrist, but it does not speak of him dying and being resurrected from the dead. It could very well indicate that he will receive a severe wound that might appear to be fatal, leading the world to assume that he has been killed. The False Prophet could then utilize that assumption to claim that he has raised the Antichrist from the dead.

The idea that the Antichrist will be a resurrected person raises a serious theological problem concerning the power of Satan. The Scriptures make it clear that the Antichrist will be Satan's man, empowered by him and possessed by him. But there is no indication in Scripture that Satan has the power to give life to anyone. Satan is not omnipotent. Jesus is the one who has "the keys to death and Hades" (Revelation 1:18).

Is The Antichrist Alive Today?

One of the most commonly asked questions is whether or not the Antichrist is alive today. I believe he is, and I believe so for two reasons. First, I believe the Scriptures teach that the generation that sees the re-establishment of Israel (May 14, 1948) will live to see all the end time prophecies fulfilled (Matthew 24: 32-34). Second, I believe the signs of the times clearly indicate that we are standing on the threshold of the Tribulation, the most important of those signs being the regathering of the Jews to their land (Isaiah 11:10-12) and their re-occupation of the city of Jerusalem (Luke 21:24).

If the Antichrist is alive today, does he know who he is? I think not. I don't think he has the foggiest idea of the role that Satan has in mind for him. He will not become the Antichrist until Satan possesses him and empowers him to deceive Europe and the Jews. His full revelation will not occur until he enters the rebuilt Temple in Jerusalem in the middle of the Tribulation and declares himself to be God.

His Character

But we are getting ahead of our story. Let's consider his character before we take a look at his career.

The Bible is very specific about the character of the Antichrist, and the picture it paints is a disgusting one. The most detailed information can be found in the book of Daniel. Consider the chart on the next page.

Characteristics of the Antichrist

Description	Little Horn Dan. 7	Small Horn Dan. 8	Willful King Dan. 11	Man of Lawlessness 2 Thess. 2
Braggart / Egotist	✔	✔	✔	✔
Blasphemer of God	✔	✔	✔	✔
Contemptuous	✔	✔	✔	✔
Persecutor of Believers	✔	✔		
Insolent		✔		
Deceptive / Shrewd		✔		
Demonic		✔		✔
Destructive		✔		✔
Willful		✔	✔	
Sexually Perverted			✔	
Militarist			✔	
Materialist			✔	

Over and over emphasis is given to the Antichrist's mouth. He will boast nonstop about himself (Daniel 7:8). He will "speak monstrous things against the God of gods" (Daniel 11:36). He will be "given a mouth speaking arrogant words and blasphemies" (Revelation 13:5). First and foremost, he is going to be a braggart and a blasphemer.

He will be strong-willed and reckless in his determination to have his way. He will show contempt for human traditions and will, of course, change even the calendar so that it will no longer be related to the birth of Jesus (Daniel 7:25).

Another point that is emphasized repeatedly is that the Antichrist will be possessed by Satan, just as Judas was (Luke 22:3). Daniel says his power will be mighty, "but not by his own power" (Daniel 8:24). Paul says his coming will be "in accord with the activity of Satan, with all power and signs and false wonders" (2 Thessalonians 2:9). John says that Satan will give his power and authority to the Antichrist (Revelation 13:2).

Because he will be demonized, he will be a man who cannot be trusted. Psalm 52:2 says he will be a "worker of deceit." Psalm 55:21 says his speech will be "smoother than butter" but his heart will be filled with war. Psalm 5:6 calls him "a man of bloodshed and deceit." In Psalm 43:1 he is referred to as a "deceitful and unjust man."

Daniel indicates that he will be a sexual pervert, most likely a homosexual. As Daniel puts it, the Antichrist will show no regard "for the desire of women" (Daniel 11:37).

The overall picture is that of an ego-maniac who abhors God and exploits people for his own purposes. He is deceptive and ruthless. He is a man devoid of integrity. This is probably the reason that when Jesus returns, John characterizes Him as the "Faithful and True" One (Revelation 19:11), in contrast to the Antichrist who has been both unfaithful and untrue.

The lack of character that will be displayed by the Antichrist is perhaps best summed up in some of the names given to him in the Scriptures:

The Beast — Revelation 13:1

The Man of Lawlessness — 2 Thessalonians 2:3

The Son of Destruction — 2 Thessalonians 2:3

The Despicable Person — Daniel 11:21

The Willful King — Daniel 11:36

The Worthless Shepherd — Zechariah 11:17

The Insolent King — Daniel 8:23

The Abomination — Matthew 24:15

The Rise of the Antichrist

The Rapture of the Church is the event that will launch the career of the Antichrist. This is revealed in 2 Thessalonians 2 where Paul states that the Antichrist cannot be revealed until "he who now restrains" him is "taken out of the way" (verse 7). The restrainer of evil in the world today is obviously the Holy Spirit, and the Spirit performs that task by working through the Church.

It is the Church that will be "taken out of the way," not the Holy Spirit. We know this for certain because the book of Revelation teaches that a great multitude will be saved during the Tribulation (Revelation 7:9-14), and no one can be saved apart from the witness of the Spirit (John 6:44, John 15:26, and 1 John 5:7). The Spirit will remain in the world, but the agency the Spirit currently works through to restrain evil, the Church, will be removed.

The Rapture itself is likely to be the event that will catapult the Antichrist to power. This is because the Rapture will produce international chaos and panic. The Antichrist, energized by Satan (Daniel 8:24), will seem to have all the answers to the world's problems. He will take over the European Union through skillful intrigue (Daniel 8:23) and will establish his headquarters in Rome (Revelation 17:3, 9,18).

The seven year time period of the Tribulation will actually begin when the Antichrist negotiates a treaty that will bring true peace to the Middle East, enabling the Jews to rebuild their Temple (Daniel 9:27). With his European base consolidated and peace achieved in the Middle East, he will set forth to subdue the whole world.

Resistance to the Antichrist

One of the myths about the Antichrist that has developed in modern day interpretation is that the whole world will become so enamored with him that all the nations will surrender their sovereignty to him voluntarily. The Bible does not teach this. It is also contrary to common sense. Africa and Asia and Latin America have not spent a century casting off European colonialism in order to suddenly turn around and receive a European dictator with open arms.

The world will resist him, and the result will be a Third World War in which he "will destroy to an extraordinary degree" (Daniel 8:24). This war will initially result in the death of one-fourth of humanity, or 1.5 billion people in today's terms (Revelation 6:2-8). As the Tribulation approaches its mid-point, this war will escalate into a nuclear holocaust that will result in the deaths of an additional one-third of those still alive — another 1.5 billion (Revelation 8 and 9).

It will be an empty victory because in the process of his conquest, one-third of the earth will be destroyed and half its population will be killed. He will then consolidate his "victory" by instituting a one-world economy and a one-world religion.

The Antichrist's One World Government

The key to his economic control will be a mark that each person will have to bear on their right hand or on their forehead (Revelation 13:16-18). No one will be able to buy or sell unless they have this mark. The mark will consist of "either the name of the beast or the number of his name" (Revelation 13:18).

His religious control will be exercised by the False Prophet who will head up his pagan religious system (Revelation 13: 11-15). He will force all of humanity to worship the Antichrist. He will be a deceiver who will astound people with "great signs" that appear miraculous in nature. In order to consolidate this Satanic religious system, the Antichrist will launch a great persecution of all those who have placed their faith in the true God since the Rapture of the Church (Revelation 12:13-17). The result will be a mass slaughter of believers (Revelation 7:9-14).

This means that by the mid-point of the Tribulation, the Antichrist will have killed more than half of humanity (1.5 billion in the seal judgments, 1.5 billion in the trumpet judgments, and an undetermined multitude of saints). It is no wonder that he is referred to in Scripture as "the man of lawlessness" and "the son of destruction" (2 Thessalonians 2:3).

The Antichrist's Possession by Satan

Nor will all this slaughter satisfy his blood thirst. About the time that the Antichrist has consolidated his world empire, Satan will be cast from Heaven and will come to earth in "great wrath, knowing that he has only a short time" (Revelation 12:12). At that point he will possess the Antichrist, even as he possessed Judas (Luke 22:3).

When the Antichrist becomes Satan incarnate, he will become a megalomaniacal tyrant obsessed with two things: himself and the Jewish people.

He will suddenly march into the rebuilt Temple in Jerusalem, stop the sacrifices, blaspheme God, and declare himself to be the one and only true God (Daniel 9:27 and 2 Thessalonians 2:4). And when the Jews reject this horrible blasphemy, he will turn on them and seek to annihilate them. This will be his all-consuming passion during the second half of the Tribulation. That's why Jesus told the Jews that this period of time would be the "great tribulation" (Matthew 24:21) — not because it would be worse than the first half, but because the wrath would be focused upon them as a nation and a people.

Satan has an insane hatred for the Jews. He hates them because they gave the world the Scriptures. He hates them because God sent the Messiah through them. And he hates them because God has promised that He will bring a great remnant of them to salvation in their Messiah. He wants to destroy them so that God cannot keep that promise.

During the second half of the Tribulation, he will almost succeed in accomplishing this goal. We are told in Zechariah 13:8-9 that two-thirds of the Jewish people will die during this holocaust (another 9.3 million people).

The Fate of the Antichrist

The Bible indicates that as the Antichrist becomes obsessed with the Jews, he loses interest in his worldwide empire, and segments of that empire begin to revolt. The core of the revolt is centered in the Asian nations who raise an army of 200 million and send it marching across Asia toward Israel where they hope to engage the Antichrist in a decisive battle for their freedom.

Daniel says that while the Antichrist and his armies are rampaging around the Middle East, looting the nations and killing the Jews, the Antichrist suddenly hears "rumors" that "disturb him" (Daniel 11:40-44). He evidently hears about the great Asian army coming to challenge him. He responds by consolidating his forces "between the seas and the beautiful Holy Mountain" (Daniel 11: 45). This is the same area that is referred to in Revelation as the Valley of Armageddon.

We are told that the Euphrates River dries up at this time and the great Asian army crosses to engage the Antichrist and his armies in battle (Revelation 16:12). As they prepare to fight, the Lord Jesus Christ breaks from the heavens, returns to the Mount of Olives in Jerusalem, and speaks a supernatural word that causes all the armies to drop dead in their tracks. "Their eyes rot in their sockets and their tongues rot in their mouths" (Zechariah 14:12), and the valley is filled with blood up to the horses' bridles for a distance of two hundred miles (Revelation 14:20).

Paul says the Antichrist will be slain by "the breath of the Lord" (2 Thessalonians 2:8). John says the Lord will make war against the Antichrist "with the sword of His mouth" (Revelation 2:16). Daniel says the Antichrist's "dominion will be taken away, annihilated and destroyed forever" (Daniel 17:26). Daniel also says that the Antichrist will be thrown into "the burning fire" (Daniel 7:11).

John confirms the fate of the Antichrist in Revelation when he says that both the Antichrist and the False Prophet will be thrown into "the lake of fire which burns with brimstone" (Revelation 19:20) where "they will be tormented day and night forever and ever" (Revelation 20:10). This means that the Antichrist and the False Prophet will be the first occupants of Hell. (Satan will not be confined there until the end of the Millennium — Revelation 20:10.)

Our Hope

The good news for believers is that we will not have to experience the horror of the Antichrist.

We are never told to watch for the Antichrist; rather, we are told to look for Jesus Christ. In 1 Thessalonians 1:10 we are assured that we who are believers are waiting for Jesus to return to "deliver us from the wrath to come." That is a glorious promise. That's why Paul calls the Rapture our "blessed hope" (Titus 2:13), and it's also the reason that he tells us to "comfort one another" with the promise of the Rapture (1 Thessalonians 4:18).

PART 2
A PROPHETIC FORUM ABOUT THE ANTICHRIST

> "[The Antichrist] shall afterwards be characterized by all manner of wicked deeds of inhumanity and lawlessness, as if to outdo all the unjust and impious men who have gone before him. He shall display against all men, and especially against us Christians, a spirit that is murderous and most cruel, merciless and wily . . . and then he shall be destroyed by the glorious second coming from heaven of the only-begotten Son of God, our Lord and Savior Jesus, the true Christ, who shall destroy him with the breath of his mouth and deliver him over to the fire of Gehenna" — Cyril of Jerusalem, *Catechetical Lectures* 15:12.

Cyril of Jerusalem (ca. 313 – 386) was a distinguished theologian of the early Church. It is believed that he was born and raised in Caesarea Maritime. He became a priest and was later appointed as the Bishop of Jerusalem.

INTRODUCTION TO THE FORUM

People who know anything at all about Bible prophecy are fully aware of the fact that there are vast differences in prophetic interpretation, based mainly on whether or not prophecy is interpreted symbolically or for its literal, plain-sense meaning. Thus, there are three major end time view-points that differ radically from each other — namely, the Premillennial, the Amillennial, and the Postmillennial.

The Premillennial view is the one I personally believe is the most biblical. It takes the Scriptures for what they say, and they say literally that Jesus will return to this earth at the end of the Great Tribulation and will reign over all the world for one thousand years. Thus, His return will be *before* the Millennium begins. The Amillennial view spiritualizes the Scriptures and argues that the Millennium began at the cross and will continue until the Second Coming of Jesus. In other words, we are in the Millennium *now*. The Postmillennial view also spiritualizes prophecy and concludes that the Church will take over the world and reign for a thousand years, at which time the kingdom will be delivered to Jesus. He is thus viewed as returning *after* the Millennium.

What people are not often aware of is the fact that there are differences of opinion within each viewpoint. For example, although most Amillennialists believe in a Heaven that is spiritual in nature, there are some who believe that Heaven will be very tangible in the form of a new earth. Likewise, among Postmillennialists, some believe the Church will conquer the world through the preaching of the Gospel, whereas others believe it will occur through political activism.

Those who believe that Bible prophecy means what it says and therefore believe it should be interpreted for its literal, plain-sense meaning also disagree among themselves over many details. The reason, of course, is that Bible prophecies are not always crystal clear as to their meaning. Literal interpreters (Premillennialists) agree on the fundamentals of the end time scenario that is presented in prophecy — that there will be a Tribulation of 7 years dominated by a tyrant called the Antichrist; that the Antichrist will be defeated by Jesus Christ at His Second Coming; and that Jesus, together with His saints, will rule over all the earth for a thousand years.

The details regarding these events are often hotly debated among prophecy scholars who interpret prophecy literally. Here are some of the areas where you will find a variety of opinions regarding end time events:

1) Will the Rapture of the Church occur before, during, or near the end of the Tribulation?

2) Will the invasion of Israel pictured in Ezekiel 38 and 39 take place before the Tribulation or during it?

3) Are the events in the book of Revelation presented in chronological order, or are they overlapping or perhaps even circular?

4) Can a person be saved during the Tribulation who heard and rejected the Gospel before the Tribulation began?

5) Is the Asian army of 200 million a real army, or is it a supernatural demonic army?

6) Is the war portrayed in Revelation 8 and 9 a conventional one, or is it a First Century man's description of a nuclear holocaust?

7) Will Elijah and Moses be the Two Witnesses of Revelation 11, or will they be Elijah and Enoch? Or, could they be two prophets selected by God from among the Tribulation believers?

8) Will the marriage feast of the Lamb occur in Heaven before the Second Coming of Jesus, or will it occur on earth after His return?

The questions go on and on, and there are a variety of opinions in response to each one. The same is true of the Antichrist. All who interpret prophecy for its plain-sense meaning agree that the Tribulation period will be dominated by a blood-thirsty tyrant known as the Antichrist. But they disagree regarding his origin and some of the events associated with his life.

To illustrate the variety of opinions, I submitted five questions regarding the Antichrist to 22 Bible prophecy scholars and teachers. The five questions were as follows:

1) Will the Antichrist be a Jew?

2) Could the Antichrist be a Muslim?

3) Will the Antichrist be killed and resurrected from the dead?

4) Where will the Antichrist's headquarters be located?

5) Is the Antichrist alive today?

As we consider each question, I will not give the answer of each person because many of the answers were the same. I will highlight the answers that were different, and I will focus on points made that were particularly insightful. At the end of the discussion of each question, I will present you with a summary of how the 22 persons responded.[1]

But before we consider the five questions, let me introduce you to the persons who participated in the forum.

The Participants

Daymond Duck — Humorous author of many basic guides to understanding Bible prophecy, including *Revelation for the Biblically-Inept, Daniel for the Biblically-Inept*, and *Revelation for Teens.* Known for his capacity for in-depth biblical analysis. He is a native of Tennessee. His ministry is called Prophecy Plus.

Gary Fisher — Established Lion of Judah Ministries in 1994 after a career as an electronic technician. Conducts meetings and conferences and hosts tours to the Holy Land. Publishes a newsletter about how current events relate to Bible prophecy. His ministry is based in Franklin, Tennessee.

Gary Frazier — Founder and director of Discovery Worldwide Ministries in Hurst, Texas. He is a recognized expert on the nation of Israel, having visited the country more than 100 times. He organizes and speaks at Left Behind Prophecy Conferences all over the nation, together with Tim LaHaye and Ed Hindson. He is also the author of several books about Bible prophecy.

Arnold Fruchtenbaum — Born in Russia of Jewish parents who migrated to the States in 1958. Founder and director of Ariel Ministries in San Antonio, Texas. He is a scholarly writer, best known for his book, *Israelology: The Missing Link in Systematic Theology.* This book was based upon his doctoral dissertation at New York University.

Ray Gano — Founder and director of an Internet Bible prophecy magazine called *Prophezine*. In addition to in-depth articles about Bible prophecy, the Prophezine website provides daily updates on prophecy in the news and provides Internet radio shows. His ministry is located in the Hill Country of Texas.

Phillip Goodman — Vice president of Thy Kingdom Come Ministries for many years before forming his own prophetic ministry in 2011 called Bible Prophecy As Written. He is a frequent speaker at Bible prophecy conferences, and he hosts a large conference each year. He is the author of a well respected book about the Antichrist that is titled *The Assyrian Connection*. His ministry is based in Tulsa, Oklahoma.

Al Gist — A former petroleum engineer who became a Baptist pastor and served in that capacity for several years before forming a Bible prophecy ministry in 2000 called Maranatha Evangelistic Ministries. He holds meetings at churches and conducts tours of Israel. His ministry is located near DeRidder, Louisiana.

Ed Hindson — President of World Prophetic Ministry and Bible teacher on "The King Is Coming" telecast. He is also the Assistant Chancellor and Dean of the Institute of Biblical Studies at Liberty University in Virginia. He is a highly respected writer and a frequent conference speaker. He has written a book about the Antichrist that is titled, *Antichrist Rising*.

Mark Hitchcock — Pastor of Faith Bible Church in Edmond, Oklahoma. He has a law degree from Oklahoma City University and a doctorate from Dallas Theological Seminary. He is a prolific writer who has produced more than 20 books related to Bible prophecy. His writings are non-speculative and are solidly Bible-based.

David Hocking — Founder and director of Hope for Today Ministries, founded in 1995 and based in Tustin, California. He has an earned doctorate from Grace Theological Seminary. He has been teaching the Bible for over 50 years and has been active in radio ministry ever since 1970. He is the author of more than 30 books, and is considered an expert on Israel in Bible prophecy.

Dave Hunt — A CPA and management consultant before directing his energies full time to Bible prophecy and Christian apologetics in 1973. Founder of The Berean Call Ministries located in Bend, Oregon. A renowned researcher and prolific writer. He retired recently from conference speaking.

Noah Hutchings — President of Southwest Radio Church Ministries, a Christian broadcasting company based in Oklahoma City that was established in 1933. He is the host of their nationally syndicated radio show "Watchman On The Wall," which is broadcast daily on stations across the United States. He is the author of numerous books and has led more than 50 tours to the Holy Land. He conducts Bible prophecy conferences all across America.

Terry James — A public relations and marketing executive for 25 years before he lost his eyesight in 1992. Since that time he has devoted himself to the study and teaching of Bible prophecy and has become a well known editor of books about Bible prophecy. He is the co-host of the Rapture Ready website, considered to be the most influential of all Bible prophecy sites on the Internet. He makes his home in Benton, Arkansas.

Nathan Jones — Web Minister for Lamb & Lion Ministries. Graduate of the Philadelphia Biblical University, with graduate work at Southern Theological Seminary. Monitors Bible prophecy in the news and edits an electronic newsletter. He also maintains a blog where people from all over the world share their views about Bible prophecy.

Tim LaHaye — Probably the best known Bible prophecy expert in the world today. Author of the best-selling *Left Behind* series of novels based on Bible prophecy. Founder of the Pre-Trib Research Center which is devoted to studying, teaching and defending the concept of the Pretribulational Rapture. His ministry is based in San Diego.

Caryl Matrisciana — A well-known expert on ancient and modern world religions, contemporary cults, paganism and the occult. Best-selling author, journalist, researcher and commercial artist. Caryl has co-produced or contributed research and expertise to more than 55 documentaries in the past 30 years. Her ministry is based in Menifee, California.

Don McGee — Vietnam War veteran, former Louisiana State Trooper, and former pastor. Established Crown & Sickle Ministries in 2002. The ministry is dedicated to the proclamation of the soon return of Jesus. Holds church meetings, speaks at conferences and edits an electronic newsletter. The ministry is based in Amite, Louisiana.

Chuck Missler — Born and raised in California. Attended the U.S. Naval Academy and was commissioned into the Air Force. Had a distinguished career in international business before becoming a Bible prophecy teacher. Founded Koinonia House Ministries in 1973. Formerly based in Idaho, the ministry has recently been moved to New Zealand. Prolific writer and frequent conference speaker.

Don Perkins — Native of Louisiana. Worked for several national ministries before founding his own ministry in 1998, called According to Prophecy Ministries, located in San Diego, California. A dynamic speaker who is in great demand for Bible prophecy conferences. Also specializes in teaching Bible prophecy at educational institutions.

Ron Rhodes — Founder and director of Reasoning from the Scriptures Ministries located in Frisco, Texas. Specialist in Bible prophecy and Christian apologetics. Author of more than 50 books. Doctorate from Dallas Theological Seminary. Adjunct professor at several seminaries. He is a frequent conference speaker.

Bill Salus — Bible prophecy researcher and writer based in La Quinta, California. Conducts an active blog at ProphecyDepot.com. Host of a weekly radio program called "Prophecy Update." Best known for his insightful book about the prophetic implications of Psalm 83, called *Isralestine*. He is also a frequent conference speaker.

Todd Strandberg — While serving in the U.S. Air Force, he established what has become the number one Bible prophecy website called, "Rapture Ready." After retiring from the military, he moved his ministry headquarters to Benton, Arkansas, where he works in tandem with his website's co-host, Terry James. He constantly monitors news events and attempts to provide interpretations of them from the perspective of end time Bible prophecy.

Question 1:
Will the Antichrist be a Jew?

In the early history of the Church, the Antichrist was usually identified as one of the Roman emperors. But after the union of the Church and State during the 4th Century, the focus of Antichrist identification shifted to the Jews, due mainly to a strong wave of anti-Semitism that swept through the Church.

Then at the time of the Reformation in the 16th Century, the Pope became the focal point of attention and derision. Repeatedly he was identified as the Antichrist. Martin Luther wrote, "The papacy is indeed nothing but the kingdom of Babylon and of the true Antichrist."[2] John Calvin echoed this opinion when he wrote, "All the marks by which the Spirit of God has pointed out Antichrist, clearly appear in the Pope."[3]

The Puritans of England strongly endorsed the idea of the papal Antichrist, and their writings influenced the Puritans in America. Increase and Cotton Mather both named the Pope as the Antichrist,[4] as did Jonathan Edwards, who wrote, "Antichrist . . . still acts under the pretense of being Christ's vicar and successor in his kingdom on earth . . . Popery is the deepest contrivance that ever Satan was the author of to uphold his kingdom."[5]

The tradition of naming the Pope as the Antichrist has continued to this day, including such modern day commentators as Arno C. Gaebelein, R. A. Torry, J. Dwight Pentecost, and Dave Hunt.

The idea that the Antichrist will be a Jew is based primarily on two scriptures — Daniel 11:37 and John 5:43. In the King James Version, the Daniel passage says the Antichrist "will not regard the god of his fathers," implying that he will not honor the God of Abraham, Isaac and Jacob. However, almost all modern translations render this verse to read, "gods of his fathers" — the word, god, being plural rather than singular. This is taken as an inference that the Antichrist will come from a polytheistic religion rather than a monotheistic one.

The other basic passage, John 5:43, quotes Jesus as saying, "I have come in My Father's name, and you do not receive Me; if another comes in his own name, you will receive him." The argument drawn from this verse is that if the Jewish people are to receive the Antichrist as their Messiah, he must be a Jew.

But what does "receive" mean? The Jewish people will certainly receive the Antichrist as a political deliverer when he negotiates a treaty ensuring their peace and enabling them to rebuild their Temple. But the Scriptures make it clear that when he enters that rebuilt Temple and declares himself to be God, the Jewish people will reject him.

Among the Bible prophecy experts I polled, there were only two who asserted a belief that the Antichrist would be a Jew. One of those was Todd Strandberg, and he based his conclusion on these two passages (Daniel 11:37 and John 5:43). The other was Ray Gano, but he used other scriptures to establish his point, and we will consider them later.

Daymond Duck, who has established a reputation for being a very meticulous interpreter of the Bible, said he has really wrestled with these two passages, and he has concluded that he could not base his decision on them since they can be legitimately translated and interpreted in different ways. He pointed instead to two other passages — Daniel 7:3 and Revelation 13:1 — in which the Antichrist is pictured as a beast coming up out of the sea. He then observed that the sea is used in Bible prophecy as a symbol of Gentile nations and, therefore, he concluded that the Antichrist will be a Gentile. David Hocking, Terry James and Nathan Jones endorsed this argument.

Arnold Fruchtenbaum, who is a Messianic-Jewish scholar, firmly believes the Antichrist will not be a Jew. He pointed to Daniel 9:26-27 which specifies that the Antichrist will be of the same ethnic identity as the people who will destroy the city of Jerusalem and its Temple. That destruction took place in 70 AD at the hands of the Romans, and thus the Antichrist, in Fruchtenbaum's opinion, must not only be a Gentile, but a Gentile of Roman origin.

Tim LaHaye endorsed this argument by Fruchtenbaum based on Daniel 9. Surprisingly, he stated that "while he [the Antichrist] might have some Jewish blood, as implied in Daniel 11:37 . . . it would be a minor factor." He pointed to the fact that it was a Roman army that destroyed Jerusalem and the Temple, and "thus I consider it quite clear that the Antichrist will be predominantly Roman. That is why Jerry Jenkins and I, in our *Left Behind* series of end time novels had him identified as being from Romania, a country that proudly claims to be from the original First Century Romans."

Ron Rhodes, a prolific writer on biblical topics, including Bible prophecy, presented the most detailed reasons for believing the Antichrist will be a Gentile. First, he pointed out that "there is no explicit statement in Scripture that he will be a Jew," whereas there is substantial evidence he will be a Gentile:

1) The strongest and clearest prophetic type of the Antichrist in the Scriptures is Antiochus Epiphanes who was a Gentile (Daniel 11:21-35). Mark Hitchcock also mentioned this argument.

2) The Antichrist is pictured as rising up out of the "sea," which is a symbol of the Gentile nations (Revelation 13:1 and 17:15). As mentioned earlier, Daymond Duck favors this argument.

3) The Antichrist rules during "the times of the Gentiles" (Luke 21:24). Phillip Goodman and Al Gist both emphasized this argument.

4) The Antichrist is said to come from the people who will destroy Jerusalem and its Temple — and therefore he must be a Gentile of Roman descent. This was the most widely used argument by all the experts.

5) The Antichrist will head up a union of European Gentile nations (Daniel 7:24). Ed Hindson also raised this argument.

Bill Salus and Mark Hitchcock both presented another observation in behalf of a Gentile Antichrist. They argued that it is highly unlikely that a Jew would mercilessly persecute the Jewish people, trying to annihilate them as the Bible clearly prophesies in Revelation 12:13-17.

Will the Antichrist be a Jew?

	Yes	No	Possibly
Daymond Duck		✔	
Gary Fisher			✔
Gary Frazier			✔
Arnold Fruchtenbaum		✔	
Ray Gano*	✔		
Phillip Goodman		✔	
Al Gist		✔	
Ed Hindson		✔	
Mark Hitchcock		✔	
David Hocking		✔	
Dave Hunt**		✔	
Noah Hutchings			✔
Terry James		✔	
Nathan Jones		✔	
Tim LaHaye		✔	
Caryl Matrisciana		✔	
Don McGee		✔	
Chuck Missler			✔
Don Perkins			✔
Ron Rhodes		✔	
Bill Salus		✔	
Todd Strandberg	✔		

*Ray Gano believes the Antichrist will be a Jew who has converted to Islam.

**Dave Hunt was incapacitated when the questions were submitted to him. His colleague, T.A. McMahon, responded to the questions in behalf of Hunt. On this question, he at first stated that he could not remember specifically what Dave's position was, but he thought Dave believed the Antichrist would be a Jew. Later, he wrote back and said that after researching Dave's writings, "it seems unlikely that he believed the Antichrist would be Jewish." Most commentators seem to have concluded that Hunt believes the Antichrist will rise out of the Catholic Church and will be a Gentile.

Question 2:
Could the Antichrist be a Muslim?

In recent years, Joel Richardson and Walid Shoebat have proposed that the Antichrist will be a Muslim. They argue that the Antichrist will arise out of the Eastern wing of the old Roman Empire and that he will head up a regional empire that will dominate all the Middle East until Jesus returns.

This theory flies in the face of the biblical statement that the Antichrist will have a worldwide kingdom and not a regional one. Revelation 13:7 states that the Antichrist will have "authority over every tribe and people and tongue and nation . . ." Richardson and Shoebat dismiss this statement as "hyperbole." There are also many other problems with this theory. Those problems are presented in detail in Part 3, Section 3 of this book.

With regard to our Bible prophecy experts, 17 of the 22 strongly denied that there is any possibility of the Antichrist being a Muslim. Of the remaining five, four of them said the Antichrist could possibly be a Muslim. Only one, Ray Gano, felt strongly that the Antichrist will be a Muslim.

Daymond Duck made the point that if the Antichrist were to be a Muslim, he would have to be an apostate one, because we are told in the Scriptures that the Antichrist will claim to be God. Such a claim is impossible for a true Muslim to make, and anyone making such a claim would incite the wrath of the Muslim world. Mark Hitchcock strongly endorsed this argument, saying, "I don't see how someone who is a follower of Islam could ever declare himself to be God."

Arnold Fruchtenbaum argued that it is not possible for the Antichrist to be a Muslim because we are told in Isaiah 28:14-22 that the Antichrist will guarantee Israel's military security through the signing of a special covenant. Arnold asserted that "no Israeli would trust any Muslim to guarantee

Israel's military security." Both Ron Rhodes and Don McGee agreed with this conclusion, as did Gary Frazier who wrote, "I do not see the nation of Israel entering into a peace treaty with a Muslim that permits the rebuilding of their Temple in light of the historical fact that the Muslims have never honored an agreement with Israel and the Quran teaches it is acceptable to lie to the infidel."

Ed Hindson strongly denied the possibility of a Muslim Antichrist. He pointed out that the Bible says the Antichrist will be a person who will not regard the god of his fathers. He then made the observation that Muslims are committed generation after generation to their belief in Allah. He adds:

> I think the New Testament makes it very clear that the Antichrist is either a total unbeliever or an apostate Christian who claims a form of Christianity but does not believe in the person of Jesus Christ . . .

Nathan Jones argued that the wars of Psalm 83 and Ezekiel 38 and 39 will decimate the Muslims in the Middle East and that this will occur either before the Tribulation or right at its beginning. He thus concluded that he cannot even imagine Islam "being a player during the Tribulation."

Tim LaHaye agreed with this observation, pointing out that "the armies of the Russo-Islamic world will be destroyed shortly prior to the signing of the covenant with Israel that will begin the seven year Tribulation." Ron Rhodes also endorsed this argument with this question: "How could a Muslim leader rise to prominence on the world scene out of the ashes of the destroyed Muslim coalition?" Gary Fisher made the same point when he observed that "if a Muslim Antichrist comes to power after these two wars, there will not be much of a Muslim army left to command." Bill Salus said he believes that the defeat of the Muslim armies will constitute "nothing less than a powerful uppercut to the jawbone of

Islam."

Nathan Jones used two other arguments to dismiss the Muslim Antichrist idea. One is the fact that the Bible says the Antichrist will declare himself to be God and will demand that he be worshiped, something "Islam would not tolerate." Jones also pointed to Daniel 11:37 which states the Antichrist will show no regard "for the desire of women." Jones said he thinks this is a clear indication that the Antichrist will be a homosexual, and "Islam has zero tolerance for homosexuality."

One of the most frequently mentioned counter arguments to the Muslim Antichrist theory is the fact that Daniel 9:26 teaches that the Antichrist will arise from the people who will destroy the Jewish Temple. That Temple was destroyed in 70 AD, and the destruction was carried out by Roman armies and not by Muslims. In fact, the Muslim religion did not even exist at that time. Daymond Duck and Terry James strongly emphasized this point.

Among those who answered that the Antichrist could possibly be a Muslim, they pointed to scripture passages that indicate he might be of Syrian descent (for example, Isaiah 10:12-19 and Micah 5:5). Others emphasized Isaiah 14:4-17 where the King of Babylon is pictured as a type of the Antichrist. Phillip Goodman strongly believes the Antichrist will come from the ancient area of Assyria, but he does not believe he will be a Muslim, although Goodman says he might be an ex-Muslim.

Only one of the Bible prophecy experts I contacted believed that the Antichrist will be a Muslim, and that was Ray Gano. He mainly based his argument on the wording of Daniel 9:26 where it says that "the people of the prince who is to come [the Antichrist] will destroy the city [Jerusalem] and the sanctuary [the Jewish Temple]." Gano argues that although it was Roman troops who destroyed Jerusalem and the Temple in 70 AD, those troops were made up primarily of mercenaries from the Middle East. Therefore, the reference to "the people of the prince" is a reference to Middle Eastern people and not to Romans.

Gano further pointed out that the prophetic types of the Antichrist which are portrayed in the Scriptures are the Assyrian, the Prince of Tyre, the King of Babylon, and the Pharaoh of Egypt. He emphasized that all of these are Middle Eastern titles, Middle Eastern names, and Middle Eastern places. Gano then asked, "If the Antichrist is to come from either Italy or Europe, why isn't he called the King of Italy or the Duke of Germany or the Prince of Rome?"

Among those who believe there is a possibility that the Antichrist could be a Muslim, Al Gist said he does not think there is sufficient evidence in the Bible to come to a conclusion on the matter. He wrote, "I am convinced he will be a Gentile, but he may or may not be a Muslim." But he went on to say that his biggest problem with the idea of a Muslim Antichrist is the fact that the Bible says he will declare himself to be God, "and I just can't see a Muslim sitting in the Temple claiming to be Allah." He then added that he believes there is solid biblical evidence that the Antichrist could be a Syrian, and most Syrians are Muslims.

David Hocking admitted that it does not seem likely that the Antichrist will be a Muslim, "but it is not out of the question." Noah Hutchings felt the Antichrist could possibly be a Muslim, and he based his conclusion on the observation that "an Israeli would not divide the land of Israel for gain, but a Muslim would." Chuck Missler simply answered, "Could the Antichrist be a Muslim? Possibly, but he will exalt himself above all that is called god, including Allah."

The chart on page 60 presents a summary of the answers received from our panel of Bible prophecy experts regarding whether or not the Antichrist could be a Muslim.

Could the Antichrist be a Muslim?

	Yes	No	Possibly
Daymond Duck		✔	
Gary Fisher		✔	
Gary Frazier		✔	
Arnold Fruchtenbaum		✔	
Ray Gano	✔		
Phillip Goodman		✔	
Al Gist			✔
Ed Hindson		✔	
Mark Hitchcock		✔	
David Hocking			✔
Dave Hunt		✔	
Noah Hutchings			✔
Terry James		✔	
Nathan Jones		✔	
Tim LaHaye		✔	
Caryl Matrisciana		✔	
Don McGee		✔	
Chuck Missler			✔
Don Perkins		✔	
Ron Rhodes		✔	
Bill Salus		✔	
Todd Strandberg		✔	

Question 3:
Will the Antichrist be killed and resurrected?

This question is based upon three statements found in chapter 13 of the book of Revelation. In Revelation 13:1-3 the author describes a beast coming up out of the sea, a beast that has seven heads. He then states that he "saw one of his heads as if it had been slain, and his fatal wound healed."

The second statement is found in Revelation 13:11-14. This passage describes a second beast coming up out of the earth with the appearance of a lamb, but who spoke like a dragon. He has the authority of the first beast, and he uses that authority to compel all people on earth to worship the first beast "whose fatal wound was healed" (verse 12).

In similar language, verse 14 presents the third relevant statement when it refers to the first beast as the one "who had the wound of the sword and has come to life."

These three statements taken together certainly give the impression that the Antichrist will be killed and then resurrected from the dead. But the overwhelming majority of our prophecy experts (17 out of 22) disagree with that impression.

Several referred to the death and resurrection of the Antichrist as a "counterfeit" (Terry James, Nathan Jones and Bill Salus). Others called it a "deceitful trick" (Ron Rhodes and Gary Frazier). In the same vein, Don McGee labeled it "fakery and trickery." Ed Hindson characterized it as "a pseudo-miracle at best."

Two of the respondents emphasized that deception is what Satan is all about. As Gary Frazier put it, "Deception is Satan's game." In like manner, Ron Rhodes referred to Satan as a "master magician, super-scientist, liar and trickster."

Regarding the meaning of Revelation 13:3, which refers to one of the seven heads of the beast from the sea experiencing a fatal wound and then being healed, Daymond Duck emphasized the fact that the verse says that the wounded head appeared "as if it had been slain." He stressed that the little word, if, makes it clear that the wound only appeared to be fatal, but was not. Don McGee made this same point and therefore argued the Antichrist will experience a resuscitation, not a resurrection.

But the most important point that the experts made about Revelation 13:3 is that it refers to only one of the beast's seven heads, and the heads represent seven world empires — namely, Assyria, Egypt, Babylon, Medo-Persia, Greece, Rome, and the final Gentile empire of history, the revived Roman empire, represented today by the European Union. Thus, the argument is that the wounded head that is healed refers to an empire and not the person of the Antichrist. It is, in fact, a reference to the death and resurrection of the Roman Empire.

This argument that the reference is to the Roman Empire and not to the Antichrist himself was made by Daymond Duck, Ed Hindson, David Hocking, Don Perkins, Ron Rhodes, and Todd Strandberg. Ray Gano also proposed this argument, but he believes the Gentile empire that the passage is referring to is the Ottoman Empire that existed from 1299 to 1923 — an empire he believes will be revived in the end times by the Islamic Mahdi.

Some, like Daymond Duck and Al Gist felt that the Antichrist would experience a serious wound of some sort, but that it would not prove fatal. Nevertheless, the world would be led to believe it was fatal.

With regards to Revelation 13:11-14, the respondents vigorously argued that any resurrection of the Antichrist would have to be a masterful deceit on the part of his False Prophet (the beast from the land). The reason for this strong opinion was their conviction that Satan does not have the power to raise anyone from the dead. God and God alone has the power of life and death. As Jesus expressed it to the Apostle John after His resurrection, "I have the keys of Death and of Hades" (Revelation 1:18).

Phillip Goodman summarized this argument succinctly when he wrote: "The Antichrist will not be resurrected from the dead because he cannot, and he cannot because God won't permit it." Goodman elaborated on this statement by pointing out that the resurrection of Jesus was to the glory of Christ (1 Peter 1:21) and the glory of God (Romans 6:4), and since God says, "I will not give My glory to another" (Isaiah 42:8), then Satan can have no part in the resurrection of anybody.

Goodman also emphasized the fact that the "proof" that Jesus really was the Son of God was "declared" in the resurrection (Romans 1:4 and Acts 17:31). The resurrection then is the cornerstone of the Gospel, and it is a glory that will be shared only with believers in Christ when they are resurrected. Goodman concluded with this observation: "For Satan to perform a resurrection . . . would dilute the power of the Gospel."

On the other side of the issue, Arnold Fruchtenbaum, Mark Hitchcock, and Caryl Matrisciana all asserted that they believe the Antichrist will be killed and resurrected. Arnold's argument was based on Revelation 5:6 where the Apostle John is in the throne room of God in Heaven and sees "a Lamb standing, as if slain." Arnold points out that the Lamb is a symbol of Jesus who actually died despite the language, "as if slain." Since the same language is later applied to the Antichrist in Revelation 13:3, Arnold concludes that it is a Greek idiom for a resurrected individual.

Mark Hitchcock said he believes Revelation 13:3 applies to an individual who is killed and resurrected, and not to the demise and revival of the Roman Empire. As to the power of Satan to raise someone from the dead, Mark believes that

"God will allow Satan to have the power to pull off this great miracle as part of the deluding influence" that will prevail in the end times (2 Thessalonians 2:11). Caryl Matrisciana agreed with Hitchcock's conclusion, writing, "I believe the Antichrist will be killed, only to be satanically revived, adding to the global delusion."

The most surprising response I received to this question about the death and resurrection of the Antichrist came from Tim LaHaye. In his *Left Behind* novels he and his co-author, Jerry Jenkins, portrayed the Antichrist being killed and later making everyone marvel as he arose from the dead. LaHaye wrote, "There are few prophetic subjects that solid Bible scholars have more disagreement on than this." He then stated that he received "much opposition" from fellow Bible prophecy experts for portraying the death and resurrection of the Antichrist in his series of novels.

He then concluded by saying that although there are good arguments on both sides of the question, "I would now opt for the whole thing to be a big fraud and his wound would be death-like, but not kill him . . . Therefore, I would now conclude that the resurrection of the Antichrist is a great deception . . ." In other words, Tim LaHaye has changed his mind on the issue since his *Left Behind* series of books were published.

Two of our respondents were uncertain about the death and resurrection of the Antichrist. Chuck Missler responded "Ostensibly, but possibly an impressive forgery." Noah Hutchings said he thinks the verses are most likely referring to the Roman Empire, but he concluded by saying, "the real meaning may not be fully revealed until it happens."

The chart on page 65 presents a summary of the answers received from our panel of Bible prophecy experts regarding whether or not the Antichrist will be killed and resurrected from the dead.

Will the Antichrist be killed and resurrected?

	Yes	No	Uncertain
Daymond Duck		✔	
Gary Fisher		✔	
Gary Frazier		✔	
Arnold Fruchtenbaum	✔		
Ray Gano		✔	
Phillip Goodman		✔	
Al Gist		✔	
Ed Hindson		✔	
Mark Hitchcock	✔		
David Hocking		✔	
Dave Hunt		✔	
Noah Hutchings			✔
Terry James		✔	
Nathan Jones		✔	
Tim LaHaye		✔	
Caryl Matrisciana	✔		
Don McGee		✔	
Chuck Missler			✔
Don Perkins		✔	
Ron Rhodes		✔	
Bill Salus		✔	
Todd Strandberg		✔	

Question 5:
Where will the Antichrist's headquarters be located?

This is a tough question. There are many scriptures that indicate that ancient Babylon, located in modern day Iraq, will be the headquarters of the Antichrist. But then, there are many indications in the book of Revelation that the headquarters will be located in Rome. There are also scriptures that state the Antichrist will go to Jerusalem in the middle of the Tribulation, enter the rebuilt Jewish Temple, and proclaim himself to be God — perhaps moving his headquarters to that city.

Complicating matters further are a whole spate of books in recent years that claim the Antichrist's headquarters will be located in either New York City or Washington, D.C.

This ambivalence is reflected in the responses of our Bible prophecy experts. A classic example is to be found in the response of Terry James. He suggested that Rome might serve as the Antichrist's political headquarters while Babylon would be his spiritual center, and his residence would be in Jerusalem.

Likewise, Arnold Fruchtenbaum proposed that Babylon would serve as the Antichrist's political and economic capital, but Jerusalem would be his religious center. Don Perkins believes Rome will be his initial headquarters, but that in the middle of the Tribulation, he will move his capital to Jerusalem.

Noah Hutchings believes there is good scriptural evidence for either Babylon, Rome or Jerusalem. He interjected the idea that from a world political viewpoint, both New York City and Washington, D.C. are good candidates. But after surveying all the options, he concluded that the headquarters will be in either Rome or Jerusalem.

Five of our Bible prophecy experts seemed uncertain about the location of the Antichrist's headquarters. Todd Strandberg focused on the fact that the book of Revelation says that when the headquarters of the Antichrist is destroyed, all the merchants of the world will mourn (Revelation 18:11). He then observed that could be Rome or a rebuilt Babylon — "so, pick your choice." Bill Salus simply stated that he is undecided, but favors Rome over Babylon. Nathan Jones wrote, "I honestly don't know for sure." He went on to explain that he definitely believes the Antichrist will rise from Rome, but he may transfer his capital to Babylon or Jerusalem. But Jones added that he "totally rejects the speculations that the headquarters could be anywhere in the United States."

Other uncertain replies came from David Hocking and Chuck Missler. Hocking's response was "I don't know." He added that all the guesses as to the location are just that — mere "guesswork." Chuck Missler presented an enigmatic response: "Daniel 11:45." That's all he said! That verse reads: "And he [the Antichrist] will pitch the tents of his royal pavilion between the seas [the Mediterranean Sea and the Sea of Galilee] and the beautiful Holy Mountain [Jerusalem] . . ." This places the Antichrist's headquarters somewhere north of Jerusalem in the Valley of Jezreel (also known as the Valley of Armageddon). Does this mean that Missler believes the Antichrist will build a new city there?

Nine of our 22 Bible prophecy experts selected the ancient site of Babylon as the political headquarters of the Antichrist, believing, of course, that Babylon will be rebuilt in the end times. All stated that they believe in literal interpretation, and therefore they believe the references to Babylon in the book of Revelation refer to the ancient Babylon located in Iraq. They reject the idea that Babylon is used as a code word in the book of Revelation for another city, like Rome.

Daymond Duck felt so strongly about this issue that he wrote several pages in response to the question. Here are some of the points he made:

1) Zechariah 5:5-11 is about a woman called "Wickedness" who represents commerce and false religion. This wicked woman is pictured as being moved to the land of Shinar (Babylon) at the end of the age. Daymond believes the woman called "Wickedness" is the same as the woman in Revelation 17 who is called "Mighty Babylon the Great Mother of Harlots."

2) Daymond argues that virtually all scholars trace the origin of false religion and world government back to the time of the Tower of Babel, and he believes that the world center of false religion and global commerce will end up in Babylon, where it started. Mark Hitchcock strongly endorses this argument.

3) There are several prophecies in the Hebrew Scriptures about the final destination of Babylon that Daymond believes have never been fulfilled. For example, Isaiah 13:4 indicates Babylon's final destruction will be by many nations whereas ancient Babylon was destroyed by the Medes and Persians.

4) Isaiah 13:5 indicates that Babylon's final destruction will be during the "indignation," which Daymond argues is another name for the Tribulation.

5) Isaiah 13:19 reveals that Babylon's final destruction will be like the destruction of Sodom and Gomorrah — suddenly, with fire and brimstone. Daymond points out that ancient Babylon was not destroyed in that manner, whereas the book of Revelation says the Babylon of the end times will be destroyed by fire in one hour (Revelation 18:10).

6) Isaiah 13:20 says Babylon will never be inhabited again after its destruction. But Saddam Hussein rebuilt some of the ancient ruins as a tourist center.

7) Daymond asserts there are many prophecies about Babylon in the Old Testament books of Isaiah and Jeremiah that are repeated about Babylon in Revelation 17 and 18. One of the many examples he gives is that Jeremiah 51:7 refers to Babylon being a golden cup in the Lord's hands, and, in like manner, Revelation 17:4 says that Mystery Babylon has a golden cup in her hand. Phillip Goodman also places a lot of importance on the connection between Old Testament promises and those contained in the book of Revelation. For example, he says that "the Babylon of Revelation 18 is semantically connected to the prophecies found in Jeremiah 50 and 51."

Mark Hitchcock stressed the importance of consistency in the interpretation of the meaning of Babylon:

> The words, Babylon, Babylonia and Chaldea are used about 300 times throughout the Bible. Now, the book of Revelation is called the Apocalypse of Jesus Christ. That means it is an unveiling; it is not a veiling. It seems odd to me that when you get to the very last couple of chapters in the Bible, all of a sudden Babylon doesn't mean Babylon . . .

Tim LaHaye reported that he has long believed that ancient Babylon would someday be rebuilt and would serve as the capital of the Antichrist's world government. He wrote, "I believe there is ample prophecy to suggest that the Antichrist will locate his one world headquarters in New Babylon and move either the United Nations there or whatever he puts together to run his anti-God, socialistic government . . ."

Eight of our Bible prophecy experts selected Rome as the political headquarters of the Antichrist. Ron Rhodes was one of these, although he stated that he thought it would be "unwise to be unbendingly dogmatic on the issue." With regard to Babylon, Rhodes said, "it is possible the Antichrist may set up a temporary headquarters there — like a satellite office — to maintain control of the world's oil wealth." Nathan Jones made a similar observation: "Babylon would be a logical location because of its proximity to the resources of the Middle East . . . It would be very smart to have a capital in the oil fields where you can defend them well . . ."

Gary Fisher focused on the statement in Revelation 17:9 that says the capital of the Antichrist will be located where there are "seven mountains." He then noted that Rome was known in the First Century as the City of Seven Hills. Caryl Matrisciana endorsed this same argument.

Ed Hindson strongly believes that Rome will be the headquarters of the Antichrist. He stated that he believes that in the book of Revelation "John is obviously using the term, Babylon, as a code word for Rome." John mentions it is the city of "seven hills," and it is the city "which reigns over the kings of the earth" — references that could only point to Rome at the time the book was written. There are also references to the city as being one where saints have been martyred for Jesus and where the prophets of God have been persecuted (Revelation 17:6).

Hindson thinks that the idea that the United Nations will be moved to Iraq is absurd. "Do you really think," he wrote, "that world leaders are going to move the headquarters of the United Nations to a site where they will have to endure suicide bombers and constant Islamic terror threats?" Hindson also emphasized the prophecy in Isaiah 13:17-20 which says that after Babylon is conquered by the Medes and Persians, it will "never be inhabited or lived in from generation to generation." Based on this prophecy and the subsequent desolation of ancient Babylon, Hindson wrote:

> Babylon has never been successfully rebuilt, and it will never be successfully rebuilt according to Isaiah's prophecy. Alexander the Great tried to rebuild it and failed. Antiochus Epiphanes tried to rebuild it and failed. Saddam Hussein tried to rebuild it and failed. And if anyone else tries to rebuild it, they will fail.

The chart on page 72 presents a summary of the answers received from our panel of Bible prophecy experts regarding where the Antichrist's headquarters will likely be located.

Where will the Antichrist's headquarters be located?

	Uncertain	Babylon	Rome	Jerusalem
Duck		✔		
Fisher			✔	
Frazier		✔		
Fruchtenbaum*		✔		✔
Gano		✔		
Goodman		✔		
Gist		✔		
Hindson			✔	
Hitchcock		✔		
Hocking	✔			
Hunt			✔	
Hutchings**			✔	✔
James***		✔	✔	✔
Jones	✔			
LaHaye		✔		
Matrisciana			✔	
McGee		✔		
Missler	✔			
Perkins****			✔	✔
Rhodes			✔	
Salus	✔			
Strandberg	✔			

*Arnold Fruchtenbaum believes that the Antichrist's political capital will be in Babylon and his religious headquarters will be in Jerusalem.

**Noah Hutchins thinks the Antichrist's headquarters will be in either Rome or Jerusalem.

***Terry James suggests that the Antichrist will have three headquarters — the political in Rome, the religious in Babylon, and the residential in Jerusalem.

****Don Perkins believes the Antichrist will start out in Rome and then move his headquarters to Jerusalem in the middle of the Tribulation.

Question 6:
Is the Antichrist alive today?

This is not a question asking for the identity of the Antichrist. Rather, the question relates to whether or not the Antichrist might be alive today, regardless of his identity.

Second Thessalonians 2:1-3 makes it clear that the specific identity of the Antichrist will not be revealed until after the Rapture of the Church. Someone had written a message to the church at Thessalonica telling them that "the day of the Lord" (the Tribulation) had arrived. This message had greatly disturbed the church because Paul had evidently taught them that the Rapture would occur before the day of the Lord. In this passage, Paul reassures the church that they are not in the day of the Lord because that day will not come until after the "man of lawlessness" (the Antichrist) is revealed.

So, Paul makes it clear that no one will know the identity of the Antichrist before the Tribulation begins. His absolute identity will become known only when he emerges as a world leader who is successful at negotiating a treaty of peace for Israel that will allow the Jewish people to rebuild their Temple (Daniel 9:27).

Again, the question is not the identity of the Antichrist, but whether or not he might be alive today.

All but two of the 22 Bible prophecy experts that were consulted agreed that the Antichrist is most likely alive today. The only persons who did not affirm the Antichrist's current existence were Arnold Fruchtenbaum and Mark Hitchcock. Fruchtenbaum simply stated: "No one knows." Hitchcock said, "I want to make it crystal clear that I don't believe anyone can say for sure that the Antichrist is alive today."

All the rest felt strongly that the Antichrist is alive today. The most common reason they gave was the accumulation of end time signs pointing to the fact that we are on the threshold of the Tribulation. As Gary Frazier put it, "The world stage is set" for the Antichrist's revealing. Todd Strandberg also stressed the accumulation of signs of the times and then stated, "Since the Antichrist would most likely be a full grown adult when he comes to power, he would have to be alive today."

Ray Gano resorted to an interesting illustration to make his point. He stated that in TV vernacular, we are currently in a "cross-fade transition." The Church is fading out and Israel is fading in, and we are currently standing in the middle of the cross-fade. Gano believes this development is a clear indication that the Church is about to be taken out and the Antichrist revealed — meaning the Antichrist must be on the scene today.

Phillip Goodman referred to "the rapid convergence of end-time-signs in contemporary history" which indicate the Antichrist must be alive and waiting in the wings to be revealed. Terry James used the same reasoning:

> Based upon all the geopolitical, socioeconomic, geophysical and religious exigencies on the scene today, I believe the Antichrist almost has to be alive and present. Israel's being front and center, the bull's eye of the Middle East peace process . . . and surrounded by enemies blood-vowed to erase them from the earth . . . makes the Antichrist's nearness almost guaranteed in my view.

Ron Rhodes followed the same path of reasoning, calling it the "convergence factor," meaning that "many ancient prophecies of the end times seem to be converging at a point in the not-too-distant future . . . and that being the case, it is quite possible that the Antichrist is in fact alive somewhere in the world today."

Tim LaHaye also pointed to the signs of the times. He wrote, "The world of ours has more signs of the Lord's return than any other generation . . . so it is certainly possible that the Antichrist is alive today." LaHaye added that "there is no indication that the Antichrist will be recognizable until after the Rapture and until he signs his special covenant with Israel, so I don't waste time looking for him. I prefer to live every day looking for Jesus . . ."

Chuck Missler made a very interesting observation that was also mentioned by Al Gist, Ed Hindson and Mark Hitchcock. It is the idea that the Antichrist has always been alive and on the scene ready to be empowered by Satan. What he means by this is that Satan has always had an Antichrist candidate available as he waits for God to execute His end-time scenario. Here's how Missler put it:

> Is the Antichrist alive today? Absolutely! He always has been. Satan has had to have a candidate in the wings, for the day is coming in which he knows he will have but little time.

Al Gist made the same point, summarizing it in these words:

> Satan does not know the exact timing of future events any more than we do. Like us, he can read the Scriptures and know about things God says are going to happen, but he doesn't know exactly WHEN they are going to happen. Therefore, I think he always has a candidate who he is preparing to become the Antichrist. When God's timetable reveals that it is time for the Antichrist to step on the scene, Satan will have his man ready.

Mark Hitchcock, who began his response by vehemently denying that anyone can say for sure that the Antichrist is alive today, proceeded to state, "I believe that Satan has a man ready in every generation — a Satanically prepared vessel to take center stage and rule the world . . . This means that Satan has someone alive today to set-up a rival kingdom to usurp the rightful place of the King of kings if the situation presents itself." On the surface, Hitchcock's response seems very confusing. It became even more confusing when he added this observation: "While I want to emphasize that I can't say for sure whether the Antichrist is alive today, I wouldn't be surprised if he is." Hitchcock concluded by explaining that the reason he believes "the Antichrist is almost certainly alive somewhere right now" is because "many of the key pieces to the prophetic puzzle seem to be lining up."

My conclusion about what appear to be very conflicting statements by Hitchcock is that he is saying that although Satan undoubtedly has an Antichrist candidate on the scene today, no one can say for sure that he will actually be the one who will ultimately become the Antichrist.

The chart on page 77 presents a summary of the answers received from our panel of Bible prophecy experts regarding whether or not the Antichrist is alive today.

Is the Antichrist alive today?

	Yes	No	Not Necessarily
Daymond Duck	✔		
Gary Fisher	✔		
Gary Frazier	✔		
Arnold Fruchtenbaum			✔
Ray Gano	✔		
Phillip Goodman	✔		
Al Gist	✔		
Ed Hindson	✔		
Mark Hitchcock			✔
David Hocking	✔		
Dave Hunt	✔		
Noah Hutchings	✔		
Terry James	✔		
Nathan Jones	✔		
Tim LaHaye	✔		
Caryl Matrisciana	✔		
Don McGee	✔		
Chuck Missler	✔		
Don Perkins	✔		
Ron Rhodes	✔		
Bill Salus	✔		
Todd Strandberg	✔		

> "[A] king shall arise out of Syria, born from an evil spirit, the overthrower and destroyer of the human race, who shall destroy that which is left by the former evil, together with himself. . . . But that king will not only be most disgraceful in himself, but he will also be a prophet of lies, and he will constitute and call himself God, and will order himself to be worshipped as the Son of God, and power will be given to him to do signs and wonders, by the sight of which he may entice men to adore him. He will command fire to come down from heaven and the sun to stand and leave his course, and an image to speak, and these things shall be done at his word. . . . Then he will attempt to destroy the temple of God and persecute the righteous people" (Lactantius, *Divine Institutes* 7:17).

Lactantius (ca. 240 – ca. 320) was an early Christian author who became an advisor to the first Christian Roman emperor, Constantine I, guiding his religious policy as it developed. He also tutored the emperor's son.

PART 3
AN IN-DEPTH LOOK
AT FOUR ISSUES

"You will be hearing of wars and rumors of wars. See that you are not frightened, for those things must take place, but that is not yet the end. For nation will rise against nation, and kingdom against kingdom, and in various places there will be famines and earthquakes. But all these things are merely the beginning of birth pangs." — Jesus in Matthew 24:6-8

THE PERSISTENT WARS OF THE END TIMES

"I looked, and behold, a white horse, and he who sat on it had a bow; and a crown was given to him, and he went out conquering and to conquer." — Revelation 6:2

Every time a war breaks out in the Middle East, I receive a flurry of phone calls and email messages asking if it could be the War of Armageddon. This question is prompted by the fact that most people are familiar with only one end time war — the one that has been popularized in movies and novels as the "Battle of Armageddon."

The concept comes from the book of Revelation where it says that armies will gather in the end times at a place "which in Hebrew is called Har-Magedon" (Revelation 16:16). This term literally means the Mount of Megiddo and refers to the ancient fortress of Megiddo that controlled the Valley of Jezreel. In English the word was transliterated as Armageddon, and the term came to be applied to the Valley of Jezreel which lies in front of Har-Magedon, running diagonally across Israel from Haifa to the Jordan River.

Most people are surprised to discover that there is no reference in the book of Revelation, or any other place in the Bible to the "Valley of Armageddon," nor is there any reference to the "Battle of Armageddon" — but more about that later. People are even more surprised to learn that Bible prophecy reveals nine wars in the end times and that Armageddon relates to only one of these.

The Next Prophetic War

Most prophetic scholars have long believed that the next great end time war will be the War of Gog & Magog that is described in Ezekiel 38 and 39. This, for example is the stated position of Joel Rosenberg in his popular book, *Epicenter*.[1] This war will start when Russia invades Israel with certain specified allies, all of whom are Muslim nations today.

But I seriously doubt that the conflict described in Ezekiel 38 and 39 will be the next war of end time Bible prophecy. There are two reasons why I feel this way.

First, there is a condition for the war of Ezekiel 38 and 39 that has not been met. Three times in Ezekiel 38 — in verses 8, 11, and 14 — it states that the war described in that chapter will not occur until the people of Israel are living "securely" in "unwalled villages."

Israel is not living in security today. It is bombarded daily by missiles from Gaza, and it is constantly under the threat of missile attacks from Hezbollah in Lebanon. There is also the ever present threat of terrorist attacks, a threat that has forced Israel to construct a 400 mile long wall down the center of the country. In short, it is laughable today to even think of the Jewish people of Israel as living "securely" in "unwalled villages."

The second reason I doubt that the war of Ezekiel 38 and 39 will be the next end time war of Bible prophecy is because the nations mentioned in Ezekiel 38:5-6 as the allies of Russia do not include a single Arab state with a border adjacent to Israel. The nations identified are Persia (Iran), Cush (most likely modern day Sudan), Put (Libya and possibly Algeria and Tunisia), and two regions that lie within modern day Turkey (Gomer and Beth-togarmah). There is no mention of the nations that share a common border with Israel — namely, Lebanon, Syria, Jordan, Egypt, and Gaza.

Why are the nations located next to Israel not mentioned as allies of Russia? I believe the best explanation of this mystery is the one supplied by Bill Salus in his book, *Isralestine.*[2] He proposes that the next end time prophetic war will be the one described in Psalm 83, a war between Israel and its neighbors. He believes this war will produce the conditions that are necessary for the war of Ezekiel 38 and 39, and I agree with that conclusion.

With that point clarified, let's now take an overview of the end time prophetic wars in their likely chronological sequence.

1) The War of Extermination
Psalm 83

This psalm states that the immediate neighbors of Israel will launch a war for the purpose of "wiping out Israel as a nation" (verse 4). The nations described as being a part of this nefarious effort are those with a common border with Israel today (verses 6-8). The rest of the psalm is a prayer for the victory of Israel (verses 9-18).

The outcome of the war is not stated, but we know from other scriptures that Israel will be victorious. For example, in Zechariah 12:6 we are told that in the end times Israel will be like "a firepot among pieces of wood and a flaming torch among sheaves, so they will consume on the right hand and on the left all the surrounding peoples . . ." Also, in Isaiah 41:12, speaking of the end times, the Lord promises Israel, "Those who war with you will be as nothing and nonexistent."

Bill Salus believes this war will result in an overwhelming victory for Israel, resulting in great territorial expansion and enhanced national resources. It will also produce the security spoken of in Ezekiel 38.

2) The First War of Gog & Magog
Ezekiel 38 and 39

But the security provided by the Psalm 83 war will not last long. The Arab nations will turn to their natural ally, Russia, and cry out for help.

And the Russians will be very happy to respond, for they have always dreamed of taking the oil fields of the Middle East. They will, therefore, launch an invasion for the stated purpose of helping the Muslims destroy Israel, but their unstated agenda will be to use the Arab invitation as an excuse to expand their sovereignty over all the Middle East. This ulterior motive is described in Ezekiel 38:12 where it says the Russians will come "to capture spoil and to seize plunder."

The invading armies will be supernaturally destroyed by God "on the mountains of Israel" (Ezekiel 39:4). The Lord will accomplish this destruction through earthquakes, pestilence, hail storms, fire, brimstone, and battlefield confusion (Ezekiel 38:19-22). Even the Jewish people will recognize that the victory belongs to the Lord, and many will open their hearts to the Lord (Ezekiel 38:23). In fact, this event could mark the occasion when the 144,000 Jews of Revelation 7:1-8 accept Yeshua as their Messiah and are sealed by the Lord for special service throughout the seven year period of the Tribulation.

The greatest mystery concerning this war is its timing. Most have placed it at the beginning of the Tribulation. Others delay its start to the middle of the Tribulation. Increasingly in recent years, the tendency has been to place it before the beginning of the Tribulation.

The best discussion of timing that has yet been written can be found in Ron Rhodes' book, *Northern Storm Rising.*[3] He concludes that it is most likely to occur 3½ years prior to the Tribulation. One of his most important reasons for this conclusion is that Ezekiel 39:9 says the Jews will spend seven years burning the weapons captured in the war, and the book of Revelation says they will be run out of the land in the middle of the Tribulation (Revelation 12:13-17). Since the middle of the Tribulation will occur 3½ years into that seven year period, that means the only way the Jews could spend seven years burning the weapons is for the war to start at least 3½ years before the Tribulation begins. (Note: The "burning of weapons" could refer to captured nuclear fuel.)

Does this mean the wars of Psalm 83 and Ezekiel 38 and 39 must occur before the Rapture? Not at all. The Rapture could occur anytime before, during, or after these wars. Keep in mind that the Rapture is not what marks the beginning of the Tribulation. The Tribulation will begin when the Antichrist signs a security treaty with Israel (Daniel 9:27). There could be a period of several years between the Rapture and the beginning of the Tribulation.

3) The Conventional War of the Tribulation
Revelation 6

The book of Revelation states that a major world war will break out soon after the Tribulation begins. This war is described in Revelation 6.

Although the Antichrist will rise to world power in Europe through cunning, deception, and intrigue (Daniel 8:23), he will have to resort to military power to conquer the world. Asia, Africa and South America have spent too long casting off the shackles of European colonialism for them to suddenly surrender their sovereignty peacefully to a new European dictator — regardless of how brilliant and charismatic he may be.

We are told in Revelation 13:7 that the Antichrist will ultimately achieve "authority over every tribe and people and tongue and nation." This authority will be achieved through war. Revelation 6 records the outbreak of this world war. It results in the death of one-fourth of humanity, or 1.5 billion in today's terms (Revelation 6:8).

The War of Psalm 83 results in the destruction of the inner ring of Muslim states around Israel. The War of Ezekiel 38 and 39 produces the defeat of the immediate outer ring of Muslim states.

But the vast majority of all Muslims live outside the Middle East, the largest Muslim nations being Indonesia (201 million), India (144 million), Pakistan (140 million), and Bangladesh (115 million). These nations are the ones who are most likely to produce the strongest resistance to a Western, non-Muslim dictator, and they will be destroyed either in this war or the one that follows it.

In other words, I believe God is going to use the Antichrist as His hammer of wrath to destroy Islam.

But many other nations in the world will also have to be subdued, and that leads us to the next war of the end times.

4) The Nuclear War of the Tribulation
Revelation 8 & 9

At some point, the book of Revelation indicates that the conventional war will morph into a nuclear holocaust, resulting in the deaths of another one-third of Mankind, or another 1.5 billion people (Revelation 9:15). This means that in the first two wars of the Tribulation, more than one half of humanity will die.

A hint that the conventional war will become a nuclear one is found in Revelation 8:7 where it states that the escalation of the war will result in one-third of the earth being burned up. Another hint is found in Revelation 16:2 and 11 where we are told that "loathsome and malignant" sores will afflict people at the end of the Tribulation, something that would be a natural consequence of radiation from the use of nuclear weapons.

It could very well be that this nuclear holocaust could be what Jesus had in mind when He stated that in the end times men will faint from fear over the expectation of the things coming upon the world, "for the powers of the heavens will be shaken" (Luke 21:26).

This war is portrayed in the book of Revelation in chapters 8 and 9 as a series of "Trumpet Judgments."

5) The War in the Heavens
Revelation 12

The next end time war is totally different in nature from all the rest. It is a supernatural one that will occur in the heavens in the middle of the Tribulation. It is prompted by an attempt of Satan to once again take the throne of God.

Satan and his angels are opposed in this war by Michael and his angels. Michael is an archangel who is pictured in the Hebrew Scriptures as the commander-in-chief of the armies of God (Daniel 10:13, 21 and 12:1). Michael and his angels prevail in this war, and Satan is cast down to earth. His access to God's throne is cut off (Revelation 12:9-10).

When this happens, Satan realizes that his time is short because he knows Bible prophecy (Revelation 12:12). In his rage, Satan decides to destroy the Jewish people, and this decision leads to the next war.

6) The War Against the Jews and the Saints
Revelation 12

Satan hates the Jews with a passion for several reasons:

1) They are the Chosen People of God.

2) God used them to provide the Scriptures to the world.

3) It was through them that the Messiah came.
4) God has promised that He will bring a great remnant of them to faith in His Son at the end of the Tribulation.

There is going to be another holocaust during the latter half of the Tribulation. When Satan is cast down to earth, he will possess the Antichrist (Revelation 13:2) and inspire him to annihilate all the Jews. This is the reason that Jesus referred to the last half of the Tribulation as "the great tribulation" (Matthew 24: 21) — not because this half will be worse than the first half, but because the wrath of Satan will be focused on the Jews.

Some of the Jews of Israel will flee to a place in the "wilderness" where they will be supernaturally protected by God (Revelation 12:13-14). Many believe this hiding place will be the ancient city of Petra, located inside a box canyon in modern Jordan. There is good reason for this assumption because Daniel 11:41 says the Antichrist will be prevented from conquering Jordan when it is part of an end time rebellion.

But Zechariah 13:8 indicates that two-thirds of the Jewish people will be killed by the Antichrist during this time, and Revelation 12:17 says the Antichrist will also war against the "offspring" of Israel — namely, those "who keep the commandments of God and hold to the testimony of Jesus." I believe this is a reference to all those who accept Jesus as their Lord and Savior during the Tribulation, both Jews and Gentiles.

It is no wonder that Revelation 7:9-14 pictures a great multitude of martyrs in Heaven, so great that it cannot be counted. They are identified as "the ones who are coming out of the great tribulation, and they have washed their robes and made them white in the blood of the Lamb" (Revelation

7:14).

So the Antichrist will be very successful in his war against the Jews and the Saints, but he will fail in his ultimate goal of annihilating all the Jews, for we are told repeatedly throughout the Scriptures that a great remnant of the Jews will live to the end of the Tribulation at which time they will receive Yeshua as their Messiah. (See: Isaiah 10:20-23; Zechariah 12:10; Romans 9:27-28; and Romans 11:25-26.)

7) The Middle East Campaign of the Antichrist Daniel 11

Daniel 11:40-45 describes a military campaign of the Antichrist in the Middle East that occurs at the end of the Tribulation.

These verses and related verses in Revelation could very well indicate that when the Antichrist becomes insanely obsessed with destroying the Jews and the Saints, the nations of the world will see an opportunity to rebel against him. The nations in the Middle East will be led by the "king of the North" (most likely Syria) and the "king of the South" (Egypt). The Antichrist responds by invading "the Beautiful Land" and subduing all the area except Jordan.

But just as he seems to be completely victorious, he hears "rumors from the East and from the North" that deeply disturb him. He retreats with his armies to the area "between the seas" where "he will come to his end." The geographical description here of a location between the Mediterranean Sea and the Sea of Galilee corresponds to the Valley of Armageddon.

I believe the rumors that frighten him are, in part, the news that "the kings from the East" (Revelation 16:12) who are bringing huge armies from Asia have arrived at the Euphrates River and are ready to cross into Israel to challenge him. The rumors from the North could relate to a reconstituted rebellious army from Russia.

8) The Battle of Armageddon
Joel 3, Zechariah 14, and Revelation 19

It appears that just as the armies from the East and the North start arriving in the Valley of Armageddon to challenge the Antichrist, the Lord breaks from the heavens, returns to the Mount of Olives, speaks a supernatural word, and all the armies are instantly destroyed.

In other words, there really is no such thing as the "Battle of Armageddon." The armies are assembled to do battle, but the Lord annihilates all of them in a microsecond "with the breath of His mouth" (2 Thessalonians 2:8).

Joel 3:16 says the Lord will "roar from Zion" and "utter His voice from Jerusalem." Isaiah 10:16 says the result will be "a wasting disease." Zechariah 14:12 says it will be a plague that will cause the flesh of the soldiers "to rot while they stand on their feet." Their eyes will rot in their sockets and their tongues will rot in their mouths. It will be like the explosion of a neutron bomb.

A Peaceful Interlude

Mercifully and joyfully, the "battle" of Armageddon will be followed by one thousand years of peace as the reign of Jesus from Jerusalem results in the world being filled with righteousness and justice (Isaiah 11:4-5,9).

Swords will be beaten into plowshares and spears into pruning hooks, and "nation will not lift up sword against nation . . ." (Isaiah 2:4). All the money that is spent today on armaments will be spent on agricultural implements. The world will be flooded with agricultural abundance (Amos 9:13). There will be no homeless or hungry people. Every man will have his own vineyard and orchard (Micah 4:4).

Satan will be bound (Revelation 20:1-3). Sin and crime will be greatly reduced. But there will be seething rebellion in the hearts of many, if not most, that are born during that time.

This is hard for most people to understand. Why would there be resentment in the hearts of people in the midst of such a perfect reign of Jesus?

The initial population of the Millennium will be all those, both Jew and Gentile, who live to the end of the Tribulation and who have accepted Jesus as Lord and Savior. All others will be consigned to death when the Lord returns. So, the Millennium will begin with only believers. But they will begin to propagate, and since death will be curtailed and life spans will be greatly extended (Isaiah 65:20), the population of the world will grow exponentially.

Those born during this time will still have the old sin nature. They will desire all the things of the flesh — booze, drugs, gambling, and promiscuous sex. But they will see that any violation of the Law of God results in swift and certain justice. Immediate arrest will be followed by an immediate trial and an immediate judgment. There will be no appeal, for all judges will be Saints in glorified bodies who will make perfect decisions. So, the average person in the flesh will say, "I love you Jesus!" but he or she will do so with clinched teeth.

The Bible states repeatedly that Jesus will rule with "a rod of iron" (Psalm 2:9 and Revelation 2:26-27). And despite the fact that His reign will produce righteousness, fairness, and perfect justice (Isaiah 11:4-5), most of those living in the flesh will deeply resent the fact that they cannot freely pursue their worldly lusts.

9) The Second Battle of Gog & Magog
Revelation 20

It is no wonder that when Satan is released at the end of the Lord's millennial reign (Revelation 20:7), the majority of those in the flesh will unite in one last rebellion against God that is pictured in Revelation 20:7-9. Led once again by Gog & Magog, this war is often confused with the war of Ezekiel 38 and 39. But the two are very different. The Ezekiel war pictures Russia coming against the nation of Israel with certain specified allies. In Revelation 20 Russia is portrayed as leading all the nations of the world against Jesus Christ.

History is going to end as it began. It started out with two people living in a perfect society, but deciding to rebel against their Creator. It ends with all of humanity living in a perfect society, and the majority making the same decision to rebel against God.

The Lesson of the Final War

One of the many purposes of the Millennium is for God to prove that Mankind's inherent sin defect can be remedied only by the Holy Spirit through faith in Jesus as Lord and Savior.

The religion of Satan has always been Humanism — the belief in Man. This philosophy teaches that Man is inherently good and is capable of perfection through education and social justice. Humanists therefore believe that if society can be perfected by supplying each person with a guaranteed job and income, Mankind will be transformed.

But the Bible teaches that Mankind is fatally flawed with a sin nature that makes people naturally evil (Jeremiah 17:9). And the Bible teaches that the only solution to the problem is the transformation of the Holy Spirit that begins when a person accepts Jesus as Lord and Savior.

God will prove this beyond doubt when He puts all of Mankind into a perfect society for one thousand years and Mankind responds in rebellion.

The Abolition of War

The Second War of Gog & Magog will be the final war of history. Following it, God will take the Redeemed off the earth and place them in the New Jerusalem He is now preparing. He will then consume the earth with fire to burn away the pollution of Satan's last revolt. Out of that fiery inferno will come new heavens and a new earth — this earth redeemed and perfected (2 Peter 3:10-13). He will then lower the Redeemed down to this earth inside the New Jerusalem (Revelation 21:2-7), and He will come to earth to live in their presence eternally (Revelation 22:1-4).

Eternal peace is coming. War is going to be abolished forever. This hope of Mankind will not be achieved by diplomats. It will be a gift of God through Jesus Christ who died to redeem Mankind and all the Cosmos. Praise the Lord!

THE LOCATION OF THE ANTICHRIST'S HEADQUARTERS

"And the woman whom you saw is the great city, which reigns over the kings of the earth."
— Revelation 17:18

Will it be Babylon, Rome, or perhaps New York City? How about Washington, D.C., or Jerusalem? All of these cities have been proposed at one time or another by students of Bible prophecy, making it clear that the Bible must not precisely identify the location.

For many years the preferred location was Rome. In recent years it has shifted to the ancient site of Babylon in modern day Iraq. But there are those who insist the location will be in the United States, in either Washington, D.C. or New York City.[1] And, as you saw in the prophetic forum in section 2 of this book, some believe it might even be Jerusalem.

Speculation about the location shifted into high gear in 2003 when the war in Iraq broke out. Wars in the Middle East always energize prophetic speculation, and that is understandable since end time Bible prophecy focuses on the Middle East and mentions several wars that will take place there.

Speculations Prompted by the War in Iraq

I must say in passing that sometimes the speculation prompted by end time wars becomes rather bizarre. For example, I was astonished to hear one of the best known teachers of Bible prophecy propose a new theory when the United States attacked Iraq. He argued that the war was a fulfillment of a prophecy in Jeremiah 50:9-10 which reads as follows:

> For behold, I am going to arouse and bring up against Babylon a horde of great nations from the land of the north, and they will draw up their battle lines against her; from there she will be taken captive. Their arrows will be like an expert warrior . . . and Chaldea will become plunder . . .

The first problem with this interpretation is that it violates the context in which the passage is found. That context is the destruction of the Antichrist's kingdom that will take place at the end of the Tribulation. The second problem is that the U.S. led coalition was anything but a "horde of great nations." We had three allies who supplied combat troops: England, Australia, and Poland. And the invasion certainly did not come from the north. It came out of Kuwait, from the southeast.

Incredibly, this prophecy teacher, who was determined to force this passage on the War in Iraq, tried to argue that the invasion really came from the north because, as he put it, "If you will check the latitude line that runs through Baghdad, you will find that it is the same one that runs through Savannah, Georgia, and thus the majority of the United States lies north of Baghdad." To say the least, I was dumbfounded by this lame attempt to twist the Scriptures to fit this teacher's preconceived idea.

The most popular new speculation that I found all over the Internet at the time the Iraqi War began was one that argued the United States is Babylon and would therefore experience an overwhelming defeat in Iraq, in accordance with the prophecies contained in Isaiah 13 & 14 and Jeremiah

50 & 51, all of which say Babylon will be destroyed in the end times. The outcome of the war put an end to this speculation.

A more credible speculation that many outstanding Bible prophecy teachers proposed was that the war in Iraq would lead to the destruction of Baghdad and the subsequent rise of Babylon as the new capital of Iraq. They then proposed that this rebuilt Babylon would become the international headquarters of the Antichrist kingdom. This speculation also failed to materialize because of the precision bombing that was aimed almost exclusively at military targets.

Speculation about Babylon

The war in Iraq was not the origin of speculation that ancient Babylon might be rebuilt and serve as the headquarters of the Antichrist. Much of the speculation preceded the war and was based on the fact that Saddam Hussein began rebuilding Nebuchadnezzar's palace in order to stimulate tourism.

As I mentioned earlier, prior to this century, the consensus of opinion among Bible prophecy experts was that the "Mystery Babylon" of Revelation 17 and the "Babylon the Great" of Revelation 18 were both references to Rome. Today, that opinion has radically shifted, and the consensus now is that these terms refer to ancient Babylon. Accordingly, these experts argue that Babylon will soon be rebuilt.

The speculation that the end time "Babylon the Great" of Revelation 18 will be ancient Babylon rebuilt is biblically based. This is the reason that Tim LaHaye, in his *Left Behind* series of books, presents Babylon as the capital city of the Antichrist's world kingdom. He and his co-author, Jerry Jenkins, portray the Antichrist moving the headquarters of the United Nations from New York to Babylon and changing the name of the organization to the Global Community.

The Argument for Babylon

Let's take a look at the biblical basis of this assumption. It begins in the Hebrew Scriptures in Isaiah 13 where the prophet says that Babylon will be destroyed in "the day of the Lord" (Isaiah 13:6,9). This terminology is a clear reference to the end times and, of course, the argument is that Babylon cannot be destroyed unless it is rebuilt.

Isaiah 14:1-17 says that the king of Babylon at the time of its end time destruction will be an oppressor of unparalleled ruthlessness. This is an image that certainly brings to mind the Antichrist.

The book of Revelation in the New Testament confirms these Old Testament prophecies. Revelation 17 associates the end time apostate world religion with Babylon. And in a similar manner, Revelation 18 associates the political empire of the Antichrist with Babylon.

Consider Revelation 18:1-10. This passage clearly teaches that Babylon will be the capital city of the Antichrist and that at the end of the Tribulation, the city will be destroyed in one hour of one day (Revelation 18:8,10).

Now, in view of these biblical passages from both the Old and New Testaments, you might wonder how anyone who takes Bible prophecy seriously could doubt that Babylon will be rebuilt and serve as the seat of power of the Antichrist. Yet, there are many outstanding Bible prophecy teachers, like Dave Hunt and Ed Hindson, who argue that Babylon will never be rebuilt and that the world headquarters of the Antichrist will be Rome.

The Argument for Rome

Let's take a look at the other side of the argument — that the Babylon of the end times will really be modern day Rome.

There are two reasons that are usually given as to why the end time Babylon may not be the Babylon of Iraq:

1) The Bible states that after Babylon is conquered by the Medes, it will become a heap of ruins and will never be rebuilt again.

2) There is strong evidence that Babylon is used symbolically in the book of Revelation to refer to Rome.

The Conquest by the Medes

With regard to Babylon being destroyed and never being rebuilt again, let's take a look at Isaiah 13:17,19,20 —

> 17) Behold, I am going to stir up the Medes against them [the Chaldeans] . . .
> 19) And Babylon, the beauty of kingdoms, the glory of the Chaldean's pride, will be as when God overthrew Sodom and Gomorrah.
> 20) It will never be inhabited or lived in from generation to generation.

This passage prophesies that Babylon will be overthrown by the Medes and that it will thereafter become a desolation, like the location of Sodom and Gomorrah. A similar passage can be found in Jeremiah 51:11.

Those who argue for the rebuilding of Babylon discount this passage for several reasons. First, they argue it is an end-time prophecy referring to the destruction of Babylon at the end of the Tribulation.

But this simply is not true. The context is clearly speaking of the conquest of Babylon by the Medes. There certainly are end time prophecies about Babylon in Isaiah 13, but this is not one of them. End time prophecies are often mixed with contemporary prophecies. For example, in Luke 21 some of the prophecies about the destruction of Jerusalem pertain to

70 AD, whereas others refer to the end times.

Also, in Jeremiah 25:11 there is a prophecy that clearly links the desolation of Babylon to its overthrow by the Medes: "'Then it will be when seventy years [of Jewish captivity in Babylon] are completed. I will punish the king of Babylon and that nation,' declares the Lord, 'for their iniquity, and the land of the Chaldeans; and I will make it an everlasting desolation.'"

Those who advocate the rebuilding of ancient Babylon usually ignore these passages that link the everlasting desolation of the city to the conquest by the Medes.

The only advocate I have seen deal with the problem did so by asserting that the reference to the Medes is really a reference to modern day Kurds who will join with a multinational force that will destroy Babylon.[2] But Babylon was conquered by the Medes, just as these prophecies said it would be, and any effort to spiritualize the prophecies to refer to modern day Kurds seems to me to be a violation of the clear meaning of the prophecies.

The Comparison with Sodom and Gomorrah

The second way people try to discount the clear meaning of Isaiah 13:17-20 is to argue that it could not refer to the Medes' conquest of Babylon because that victory was so surprising and swift that it did not result in the destruction of the city. They contend, "The passage says Babylon will be destroyed in the same manner as Sodom and Gomorrah, and that means sudden, total destruction."

It is true that the Medes conquered the city in a relatively bloodless and non-devastating manner. They did not attack the city or put it under siege. Instead, they dammed up the Euphrates River, which ran through the center of the city. Then, while the Babylonian rulers were in the midst of a drunken feast, the armies of the Medes simply walked down the dried-up riverbed, underneath the walls!

But the passage does not say that Babylon will be overthrown like Sodom and Gomorrah! That claim is based on an interpretation that the text does not justify. Read the passage carefully. It simply says that after the Medes conquer the city, it "will be as when God overthrew Sodom and Gomorrah."

And that is exactly what happened. The city was conquered by the Medes in 539 BC. Thereafter, it went into a sharp decline. By the time Alexander the Great arrived 200 years later, it was in ruins. He announced his intentions to rebuild it, but he died suddenly before he could do anything. His generals abandoned the city and moved the capital to the Tigris River where they built a new city called Seleucia.

Babylon became like Sodom and Gomorrah — a heap of ruins — and it has been in that condition ever since, just as prophesied in Isaiah 13.

Rebuilding Efforts

But those who believe Babylon will be rebuilt counter by asserting that its rebuilding was begun by Saddam Hussein. It is true that Saddam built one of his many presidential palaces there, on the outskirts of the ancient city. But he did not rebuild the city for habitation.

All Saddam did was restore some of the ruins of Nebuchadnezzar's palace as a tourist attraction. Modern day satellite photos of the site still show it to be an uninhabited heap of ruins.

There are continuing efforts to rebuild the ruins of Nebuchadnezzar's palace complex. These are headed up by The World Monuments Fund.[3] But, again, these efforts seek only to make the area a tourist attraction. There is no plan to rebuild the city for habitation.

Of course, with modern building techniques, the Antichrist could quickly build an international headquarters on the site, but Isaiah 13:20 says that once it is conquered by the Medes, "it will never be inhabited or lived in from generation to generation."

The References in Revelation

So, what about the references in the book of Revelation which clearly indicate that Babylon will be the headquarters of the Antichrist during the Tribulation? The problem is that a qualifying term is used that makes it highly questionable that the meaning is literal Babylon.

The passage is Revelation 17:5. In the New American Standard Version, the translation introduces the reader to "a mystery, Babylon the Great." The King James and New King James Versions both render the meaning as "Mystery Babylon the Great."

Either way, the use of the qualifying word, mystery, seems to indicate that Babylon is to be taken symbolically. This conclusion is reinforced by Revelation 11:8 where Jerusalem is referred to symbolically as the city "which mystically is called Sodom and Egypt." Notice again the use of the word mystically as a tip-off that the author is speaking symbolically.

In like manner, Peter uses Babylon as a symbol of Rome in 1 Peter 5:13. He was writing from Rome, and he closes the epistle by sending greetings from "the church that is at Babylon" (KJV). This statement makes it clear that among First Century Christians, Babylon was a nickname or code word for Rome.

Keep in mind that when John wrote Revelation, he was a Roman prisoner. He could not, therefore, make any disparaging references to Rome in his writings, so he used the nickname of Babylon and even emphasized that it was a code word by referring to it as "Mystery Babylon."

That John had Rome in mind is indicated later in chapter 17 of Revelation in two places. In verse 9 he refers to it as the city of "seven mountains." In the First Century context, this could only refer to Rome, which was known as "the city of the seven hills." In verse 18, John refers to the city as "the great city that reigns over the kings of the earth." Again, this could only have been Rome in a First Century setting.

Additionally, in verse 6, John refers to the city as one that is "drunk with the blood of the saints and with the blood of the witnesses of Jesus." This appears to be a clear reference to Rome which was severely persecuting Christians at the time and which continued to persecute and kill true believers throughout the Middle Ages.

What about New York City?

Another understandable speculation that has become very popular in recent years is the identification of end time Babylon as New York City. The reason, of course, is that the description of Babylon in Revelation 18 fits our nation so perfectly. Babylon is described as the world's dominant economic power (Revelation 18:11-20) and the source of worldwide immorality (Revelation 18:2-9). Her sins have "piled up as high as heaven" (Revelation 18:5), and she has "glorified herself and lived sensuously" (Revelation 18:7).

Yes, it sounds like the United States, but it is not. Keep in mind the context of Revelation 18. It is speaking of the Antichrist's empire at the end of the Tribulation. We know from the book of Daniel that the Antichrist's worldwide empire will be based in Europe, arising from the revived Roman Empire.

By the end of the Tribulation, the Antichrist's empire will have completely replaced the United States as the world's dominant political and economic power. It will also be the seat of the One World Religion headed up by the Antichrist's False Prophet (Revelation 17).

Is Jerusalem a Possibility?

Both Jesus in Matthew 24:15 and Paul in 2Thessalonians 2:3-4 indicate that the Antichrist may make Jerusalem His religious capital because it is there that he will desecrate the Jewish Temple by entering it and declaring himself to be God.

But the description of the Antichrist's headquarters in Revelation 18 eliminates Jerusalem as his governmental capital because it is described as the commercial and mercantile center of the world. Jerusalem is certainly not that now, and its isolated, inland position seems to rule out any possibility of it becoming a financial powerhouse in the future.

Concluding Thoughts

So, there you have it — a summary of arguments pro and con concerning whether or not the end time capital of the Antichrist will be ancient Babylon rebuilt, modern day Rome, or New York City. I challenge you to be a good Berean (Acts 17:10-11). Dig into the Scriptures, study diligently, and draw your own conclusions.

The important thing to keep in mind is that it doesn't really make any difference whether the Antichrist will reign from Babylon, Rome, New York City, or some other city. Regardless of which city it might prove to be, Almighty God is going to destroy the city, its king, and all its sinful activities in one hour of one day (Revelation 18:8,10).

The point is, that regardless of the true identity of Babylon, Jesus is going to triumph, and we, the Redeemed, are going to win in the end. Maranatha!

THE POSSIBILITY OF A MUSLIM ANTICHRIST

"Then the king will do as he pleases, and he will exalt and magnify himself above every god and will speak monstrous things against the God of gods . . . he will honor a god of fortresses, a god whom his fathers did not know . . ." — Daniel 11:36,38

The question as to whether or not the Antichrist will be a Jew or a Gentile has been hotly debated by Bible prophecy experts ever since the revival of the study of end time Bible prophecy some 400 years ago. In recent years the debate has taken on a new flavor due to some who are obviously impressed with the resurgence of Islam worldwide. They have developed a whole new scheme of end time events in which one of the most prominent features is a Muslim Antichrist.

For those of you interested in pursuing this topic in greater detail, I would recommend that you consult the following two books: *Antichrist: Islam's Awaited Messiah* by Joel Richardson and *God's War on Terror: Islam, Prophecy and the Bible* by Walid Shoebat with Joel Richardson.

Richardson and Shoebat

Richardson's book, which was published in 2006 is considered to be the cornerstone of the whole movement.[1] It was picked up by WorldNetDaily and republished by them in 2009 under the title *The Islamic Antichrist.*[2] WorldNetDaily has promoted the book vigorously ever since. The book features ten endorsements by various pastors, professors, and heads of ministries. Not a one is a Bible prophecy teacher or recognized expert on Bible prophecy.

Joel Richardson is a excellent writer who knows how to make a persuasive argument, particularly if the reader knows nothing about Bible prophecy.

Walid Shoebat's book is more detailed and is much longer (516 pages to Richardson's 276 pages).[3] Walid Shoebat is an outstanding speaker on the topic of Islamic terrorism.[4] But he is not a writer. His writing is very tedious and difficult to follow. Even worse, the organizational format of the book is chaotic and confusing. I can say without hesitation that his book is one of the most difficult ones I have ever tried to wade through in my lifetime of reading. To me, it was like trying to read and make sense out of the Qu'ran!

Background Information About Islam

Before I review the rather bizarre theories about the end times that are contained in these books, I think it would be wise to present some background material about Islam. I realize that you may be well informed about Islam, but I have found that even those who have studied Islam rarely know anything about Islamic eschatology.

As I am sure you are aware, the holiest book of Islam is the Qu'ran, which supposedly contains statements of the Islamic god, Allah, which were given to his prophet, Mohammad, by the angel Gabriel.

Mohammad was illiterate, so scribes wrote down what he said over a 23 year period of time, until his death in 632 AD. Much of the content of the Qu'ran was delivered to Mohammad while he was experiencing seizures that even his first wife considered to be demonic in nature. The scribes began compiling the Qu'ran shortly before Mohammad's death. The

Qu'ran is about the length of the New Testament.

The second most sacred book of Islam is called the Hadith. It is mainly a collection of Mohammad's sayings that were not considered to be revelations directly from Allah. The Hadith also contains stories about things Mohammad did.

I think it is very important to note that the Hadith was compiled in the 9th Century, about two hundred years after the death of Mohammad. There were several compilations made during that time, but the most authoritative is considered to be the one by al-Bukhari. He collected a total of over 400,000 sayings of Mohammad and stories about him. These came from the writings of both friends and family members. Many came from Mohammad's 15 wives. Al-Bukhari verified 7,000 as "genuine." These became the al-Bukhari Hadith, one of several versions of the Hadith that have been produced by other compilers.[5]

Strangely, the Qu'ran contains very little prophecy about the end times. It mainly affirms that history will consummate with what's called "the Hour." This is when the resurrection and judgment will take place. So, the Hadith, containing hearsay statements by Mohammed, is the major source of Islamic eschatology.

An Islamic Puzzle

It is extremely difficult to piece together the Islamic concept of the end times. The information is greatly disjointed, being spread throughout the Hadith. Also, unlike Christian prophecy scholars, Islamic students of prophecy have not attempted to systematize their concepts into charts and diagrams which show how all the events are related to each other.

The most helpful source I was able to discover was a book by Dr. Samuel Shahid called *The Last Trumpet*.[6] He attempts to show that the major concepts of Islamic eschatology were borrowed from the Hebrew Scriptures, the Christian New Testament, and the concepts of Zoroastrianism. The author is the director of Islamic studies at Southwestern Baptist Theological Seminary in Ft. Worth, Texas.

Dr. Shahid proves conclusively that Mohammad secured many of his ideas orally from Christians, Jews, and followers of Zoroastrianism.[7] In the process he got many of the stories and principles confused. For example, the Hadith states that the mother of Jesus was Mary, the sister of Moses!

Dr. Shahid also points out that the Hadith was compiled at a time when Islamic authorities knew much more about the Bible and Christian traditions and literature. Thus, many Hadith passages were manufactured and embellished and were heavily influenced by Christian sources.

Complicating matters is the fact that Hadith passages concerning the end times are highly contradictory, and thus it is difficult to nail down a lot of specifics. Only a general outline of end time events can be compiled.

The Islamic Signs of the Times

One very interesting aspect of Islamic eschatology is that it presents signs of the times for people to watch for. Like Christianity, Islam teaches that only God knows the exact timing of end time events. But there are signs to watch for that will indicate the season of the end times, and these signs fall into two categories: major and minor.

Most of the minor signs have to do with general trends in society. The major signs relate to specific prophesied events that will occur between the time of the appearance of the Antichrist and "the Hour" of resurrection and judgment. The listings of both the minor and major signs vary greatly.

The Minor Signs

Let me give you some examples of minor signs. As I do so, you will see how they mirror the signs prophesied in the Bible.[8]

1) An increase in ignorance concerning the fundamentals of the faith.
2) Increasing instability of the faith (Muslims becoming Christians overnight).
3) An increase in false prophets.
4) An increase in apostasy (as evidenced by Muslims following false teachers).
5) An increase in religious pretentiousness (as in the building of luxurious mosques).
6) An acceptance of astrology.
7) An increase in alcohol use and illicit sexual relations.
8) An increase in natural calamities.
9) An increase in political corruption.
10) People longing for death (due to the increase in calamities and wickedness).
11) Increasing paganism. (Muslims will increasingly follow the life-styles of non-Muslims.)
12) An increase in war and civil wars (even wars among Muslims).

There are many other minor signs that are peculiar to Islam, most of which are fantastical in nature. Here are some examples:[9]

1) Women will outnumber men by 50 to 1. (No reason is given, but it is likely due to the expectation of many

jihad martyrs in the end times.)

2) The Arabs must conquer Constantinople. (The city, now called Istanbul, was conquered by Muslims in the 15th Century, but not by Arabs.)

3) A people will emerge who eat with their tongues like cows.

4) Time will contract, with a year being like a month and a month like a week.

5) Wild beasts will speak to men.

6) The Euphrates River will uncover a mountain of gold.

The Major Signs

The major signs pointing to "the Hour" are all critical events that are part of the end time sequence of events, beginning with the appearance of the Antichrist. Muslim scholars generally do not try to present a strict chronological order of what is going to ultimately transpire, but the order presented below is representative:

1) The appearance of the Antichrist, called the Dajjal.

2) The rising of the Islamic Messiah, called the Mahdi.

3) The Return of Jesus.

4) The Reign of Jesus.

5) The Day of Resurrection, called "The Hour."

6) The Day of Judgment.

There are many other end time events mentioned in the Hadith, but these are the most important. Let's look for a moment at each of these key events in their chronological order.

End Time Specifics

1) The Appearance of the Antichrist, called the Dajjal. He will be a Jew born in Iran to parents who have been childless for 30 years. He will have only one eye. He will claim to be a prophet, and then he will claim to be divine. He will deceive many by his godliness and his miracles. He will go forth with an army of 70,000 Jews and 70,000 Tartars, and he will conquer all the world except Mecca and Medina. His reign will last for 40 days during a time when one day will be like a year. Some passages of the Hadith indicate that he will have the word "Infidel" written on his forehead. His reign is characterized by cruelty and deceit. He has a militaristic mentality. His purpose is to be deified, worshiped, and to reign.[10]

2) The rising of the Islamic Messiah, called the Mahdi. He will be a descendant of Mohammed who will come on a white horse. He will deliver the world from the reign of the Dajjal. In the process he will conquer Israel and slaughter the Jews. He will establish a new Islamic world headquarters in Jerusalem, and he will rule for 7 years (and possibly 8 or 9 years, depending upon differing Hadith passages). His rule will end with his death.[11]

3) The Return of Jesus. It is not clear at what point in the career of the Mahdi that Jesus will return. Some believe it will be as soon as the Mahdi is able to organize his Muslim army to oppose the Dajjal's Jewish army. Jesus will return to the Mount of Olives and then head to Damascus where he will meet up with the Mahdi and submit himself to him as a subordinate. At some point in the Mahdi's wars Jesus himself will be the one who will kill the Dajjal and see to the annihilation of the Jews. Jesus will then serve as an Islamic evangelist, proclaiming Islam as the one and only true religion, and he will establish Islamic Shari'ah law throughout the entire earth.[12]

4) The Reign of Jesus. Upon the death of the Mahdi, Jesus will assume control of the Islamic worldwide kingdom. He will reign for 40 years. He will be a just ruler. Every harmful beast will be domesticated. There will be abundant rain and plentiful harvests. All weapons of war will be converted into tools of agriculture, and there will be world wide peace. (All of this imagery is taken, of course, from the book of Isaiah.) Jesus will go to Mecca regularly to perform rituals of pilgrimage. Twenty-one years into His reign, He will marry and begat children. Nineteen years later He will die. He will be buried in Medina next to Mohammad where He will await the Day of Resurrection like all other humans who have died.[13]

5) The Day of Resurrection, called "The Hour." There is only one resurrection in Islamic eschatology. The saved and the unsaved are resurrected at the same time. Mohammad will be the first human being to be resurrected. All those resurrected will be naked. Abraham will be the first person to be clothed by Allah. He will be seated facing Allah's throne. Mohammad will then be clothed and will be seated at the right hand of Allah.[14]

6) The Day of Judgment. At this point Allah descends from Heaven to judge all humanity. Allah will weigh the good and bad deeds of each person. This is called the concept of "the Scale." The deeds of all people will be weighed in Allah's scales to determine their eternal destiny.[15]

The Richardson Thesis

Now, with this brief background in Islamic eschatology, let's take a look at the thesis that Richardson presents in his book.

He argues that the Mahdi will be the Antichrist of the Bible and that the Muslim Jesus will be the False Prophet of the Bible who serves the Antichrist and his purposes. Both will be destroyed when the true Jesus returns at the end of the Tribulation.[16] The true Jesus will be viewed by Muslims as the Dajjal, or the Islamic Antichrist.

As proof of his thesis, he points repeatedly to the "amazing similarities" and "amazing parallels" between the biblical Antichrist and the Muslim Mahdi.[17] He points out that both are pictured as an unparalleled political, military and religious leader who will come on a white horse and who will team up with a false prophet to conquer the world, and institute a one world religion.

The Bible says the Antichrist will change the laws and the times. Richardson asserts that the Mahdi would do just that, instituting Shari'ah law and imposing the Islamic calendar.[18] Likewise, the Bible says the Antichrist will behead those who resist him, and Richardson spends an entire chapter emphasizing that execution by beheading is one of the cardinal characteristics of Islam.[19]

Richardson even points out that there is a Hadith passage that states the Mahdi will make a covenant with the Romans through a Jewish intermediary and that the covenant will be for a period of seven years, just like the seven year covenant the Bible says the Antichrist will make with the Jewish people.[20]

The Similarities Between Islamic and Biblical Prophecies

I personally find nothing startling or surprising about these similarities. As I have already pointed out, Mohammed got most of his ideas concerning the end times from discussions with Christians and Jews. And these ideas were later embellished by his followers who were even better acquainted with biblical prophecies concerning the end times. Furthermore, the one who inspired Mohammed and his followers, namely Satan, is an expert on Bible prophecy!

Nor am I impressed with the similarities he points out. It is only natural that the Mahdi, like the Antichrist, should be viewed as a great leader who will conquer the world and institute a one-world religion. The assertion that the Mahdi will return on a white horse is, of course, borrowed directly from Scripture, as is the idea of the False Prophet.

As for the laws and the calendar, whoever the Antichrist may be, it is certain he will change the laws by instituting a totalitarian system devoid of individual rights, and he will most certainly change the calendar because the calendar followed by most of the world dates from the birth of Jesus.

The point about beheading is flimsy evidence at best. Beheading is not a unique characteristic of Islam. It was one of the stellar characteristics of the French Revolution, and is just the type of horror the Antichrist would institute, regardless of his nationality or religion.

And as for the seven year covenant, the Mahdi makes it with the Romans (which Richardson says should be interpreted as Christians). It is not a covenant with the Jewish people, as the Bible prophesies.

Richardson's End Time Scenario

According to Richardson's end time scenario, the Mahdi and the Muslim Jesus (the False Prophet) will unite the whole Islamic world, reviving the Ottoman Empire.[21] They will conquer Israel and establish the headquarters of the Caliphate in Jerusalem. Their rule will come to an end with the Battle of Gog & Magog that is portrayed in Ezekiel 38 and 39, which will occur at the end of the Tribulation, when the Lord Jesus Christ returns. And, again, when Jesus returns, the Islamic world will view the true Jesus as the Dajjal, or the Islamic Antichrist.

One glaring problem with this scenario is that Islamic eschatology teaches that the Dajjal, the Antichrist, will come first, and his appearance will signal that the Mahdi is about to arise.[22] Richardson's scenario puts the appearance of the Islamic Dajjal at the end of the Tribulation instead of at the beginning. And so, I ask, "If some person arrives on the scene claiming to be the Mahdi before the appearance of the Dajjal, why would he be accepted by Muslims?"

Contradictory Concepts of the Mahdi

Nor is it likely that any person claiming to be the Mahdi would be immediately accepted by the whole Islamic world. The reason is that the concept of the Mahdi is one of the key elements in Islamic eschatology that separates the Shi'ites from the Sunnis.[23]

The Sunni branch of Islam believes that Mohammed's successor, Abu Bakr, selected in 632, rightfully took his place as the leader of the Muslim world. The Shi'ites, on the other hand, believe that Mohammed's successor should have been a blood relative and not just a person selected on the basis of Islamic piety or politics. Abu Bakr was Mohammed's father-in-law. The Shi'ites favored Ali ibn Abi Talib, the prophet's cousin and son-in-law. Ali ultimately became the fourth successor of Mohammed, reigning from 656 to 661.

After the death of Ali, his heirs were overcome by a military leader named Mu'awiya Umayyad, who proceeded to establish the Umayyad Dynasty centered in Damascus. Shi'ites refused to recognize his leadership since he was not a blood relative of Mohammed. They looked, instead, to the surviving heirs of Ali for their leadership.

The blood line of Mohammed through Ali became extinct in 873 A.D. when the last Shi'ite Imam, Muhammad al-Mahdi, who had no brothers, disappeared within days of inheriting the title at the age of four. The Shi'ites refused to accept that he had died or been killed, preferring to believe that he was merely "hidden" and would one day reappear.

This event is referred to in Shi'ite theology as "The Great Occultation" (the hiding).[24] This boy was the Shi'ite's Twelfth Imam, and he is the one they expect to return as the Islamic Mahdi. The Sunnis strongly reject this concept, particularly since many Shi'ites teach that the Twelfth Imam will declare that the Shi'ite version of Islam is the orthodox version.

Islamic historian Timothy Furnish has summed up the difference between the two groups concerning the Mahdi by observing: "For Shi'ites he has already been here, and will return from hiding; for Sunnis he has yet to emerge into history: a comeback versus a coming out, if you will."[25]

The Mahdi being heralded by Mahmoud Ahmadinejad in Iran is the Twelfth Imam. If he were to suddenly appear, he would be rejected by Sunnis, and the Sunnis constitute 90% of all the Muslims in the world.

God's Covenant with Ishmael

Another problem with the idea that the Mahdi will unite the Muslim world is that the whole idea is contradictory to one of the promises God made in His covenant with Ishmael (Genesis 16:10-12). In that covenant, in which God promised that the descendants of Ishmael would be greatly multiplied and would be given all the land east of Israel, God also stated that the Arab peoples would be like wild donkeys for they would always be in conflict with each other.

As Jacob Prasch has pointed out in his writings on this subject, this aspect of the covenant with Ishmael has been manifested throughout history to this day through the internecine wars between the Arabs.[26] They fought each other for centuries in pre-Islamic Arabia. Mohammed believed that he could unite them through the advocacy of a monotheistic religion, but he failed. Sunnis and Shi'ites have hated and warred with each other since the 8th Century. Consider the modern day war between Iran and Iraq, and the Iraqi invasion of Kuwait, with the intent of conquering all the Middle East.

Prasch sums up the problem of Arab unity by declaring, "The curse of Genesis prevents Islamic unity from developing a united empire over-running the West."[27] He further observes: ". . . the greatest Islamic Empire was strategically dominated by Ottoman Turks who subjugated the Arab Moslems as serfs and slaves . . ."[28]

The Extent of the Antichrist's Kingdom

One of the most peculiar aspects of Richardson's end time scenario is his insistence that the Mahdi's revived Ottoman Empire will be a regional one and not a worldwide one as is claimed in both Islamic and biblical prophecy.

In order to sustain this totally revisionist interpretation of end time prophecy, Richardson goes to great pains to deny the clear meaning of Revelation 13:7 which reads as follows: "And it was given to him [the Antichrist] to make war with the saints and to overcome them, and authority over every tribe and people and tongue and nation was given to him."

Let me ask you a question: What more would God have to say to convince us that the Antichrist will have a worldwide kingdom?

Yet, Richardson tries to dismiss this verse as nothing but hyperbole. He does so by quoting Daniel 5:18-19 where it says that Nebuchadnezzar, was feared by "all peoples and nations and men of every language." Richardson then asks, "Did every single nation in the earth fear Nebuchadnezzar?"[29] My answer would be, "Yes, all nations that were aware of him." That's all the statement means in its context.

Richardson then quotes 1 Kings 4:34 which says that men of all nations came to listen to Solomon's wisdom, "sent by all the kings of the world, who had heard of his wisdom." He then asks derisively, "Was Solomon's wisdom so impressive that not a single king in all the earth failed to hear of it?"[30] That's not what the verse says. Read it again. It says the kings who had heard of his wisdom sent representatives — not all kings.

Context determines meaning, and the context of Revelation 13:7 clearly means that the Antichrist kingdom will be worldwide, not just a regional coalition of Muslim nations. Richardson's attempt to limit the kingdom of the Antichrist to a regional area is reminiscent of the attempt of Genesis revisionists to limit the worldwide flood of Noah to the Middle East.

Furthermore, the worldwide nature of the Antichrist's kingdom is affirmed in Daniel 7:23 where the prophet states that the Antichrist will "devour the whole earth and tread it down and crush it." Richardson ignores this verse.

The Revived Ottoman Empire

Richardson's claim that the final Gentile empire of the Antichrist will be the revived Ottoman Empire forces him to deal with Nebuchadnezzar's vision of Gentile kingdoms, recorded in Daniel 2:31-45. The traditional interpretation of that vision is that its succession of empires ends with the Roman and that it is the Roman Empire that will be revived in the end times and provide the platform from which the Antichrist will arise.

To accommodate his thesis, Richardson argues that the Roman Empire continued to exist in the form of the Byzantine Empire until 1453 when it fell to the Ottoman Empire. It is therefore the Ottoman Empire, which ceased to exist in 1923, that will be resurrected in the end times, and not the Roman Empire, and thus the Antichrist will arise out of the revived Ottoman Empire.

The first problem with this interpretation is that it denies the historical fact that the Roman Empire ceased to exist in 476 with the collapse of Rome. What was left of the empire in the East, which is referred to by modern historians as the Byzantine Empire, was Roman in name only, reminiscent of The Holy Roman Empire that existed in the Germanic areas of Europe from 800 to 1806, a political entity that Voltaire characterized as "neither holy, nor Roman, nor an empire."[31]

Another problem is that Nebuchadnezzar's dream does not provide for the insertion of the Ottoman Empire. The head of gold stood for the Babylonian Empire; the chest of silver for the Medo-Persian Empire; the thighs of bronze for the Greek Empire; and the legs of iron for the Roman Empire. The feet of iron mixed with clay represent the final Gentile empire out of which the Antichrist will arise. The traditional interpretation has been that the feet stand for a revival of the Roman Empire.

But if the Ottoman Empire is to be inserted into the picture following the Roman, where is the symbol of it? Do the feet represent both the Ottoman Empire and its end time revival? There just are not enough body parts to provide symbols for both the Ottoman Empire and its revival.

The same problem occurs when you consider Revelation 17:10-11. In this passage the Apostle John is told that there are seven kings or empires to be considered in world history and that "five have fallen, one is, the other has not yet come; and when he comes, it must remain for a little while. And the beast which was and is not, is himself also an eighth, and is one of the seven, and he goes to destruction."

At that point in history, the five fallen would have been Egypt, Assyria, Babylon, Medo-Persia, and Greece. The one existing would have been the Roman. The one to come would be the revival of the Roman, out of which the eighth and final empire, the worldwide kingdom of the Antichrist would arise.

If you insert the Ottoman Empire into this list, where does it fit? If it is the seventh, then its revival would be the eighth, and there is no place left for the final worldwide empire of the Antichrist. I suspect this is the reason that Richardson insists that the revival of the Ottoman Empire will be the final empire out of which the Antichrist will arise, and that it will not develop into a worldwide empire, as both Islamic and biblical prophecies specify. There just are not enough empires mentioned in Revelation 17 to include the Ottoman Empire, its resurrection, and its evolution into the final worldwide empire of the Antichrist.

Another problem with Richardson's Ottoman Empire thesis is that he completely ignores the prophecy in Daniel 9:26 that says the Antichrist will arise out of the people who will destroy the Jewish Temple. It was the Romans who destroyed the Temple in 70 AD, and it is from the Romans that the Antichrist must come. To me, it is just incredible that Richardson would totally ignore this prophecy.

The War of Gog & Magog

The final problem with Richardson's thesis that I would like to mention concerns his interpretation of the War of Gog & Magog that is pictured in Ezekiel 38 and 39.

Richardson denies that the war described in Ezekiel 38 and 39 will be led by Russia or that Russia will even have a part in it. Of course, he has to take this position since he argues that the invading force will be the revived Ottoman Empire, which Russia was never a part of.

He says that the only reason people have ever included Russia as part of the invading armies is because Ezekiel says the invasion will be led by the prince of Rosh, and that the word, Rosh, sounds like Russia.[32] This assertion is, of course, patently false. Many authors, including Mark Hitchcock and Ron Rhodes have gone to great pains to present historical evidence that identifies Russia with Rosh.[33]

The passage in question, Ezekiel 38:2, says the invasion will be led by "Gog of the land of Magog, the prince of Rosh, Meshech, and Tubal . . ." It is important to note that both Josephus in the First Century and Jerome in the Fifth Century identified Magog with Scythian tribes in Russia.[34]

Richardson favors Turkey as the leader of the coalition.[35] Yet, Ezekiel 38 clearly states that the invasion will be led by the Prince of Rosh coming from "the remote parts of the north" or "the uttermost parts of the north" (Ezekiel 38:15). There is no way that Turkey could be considered a nation located in "the remote parts of the north." Again, this is a verse that Richardson completely ignores.

Richardson never reveals when he believes the Ezekiel 38 invasion of Israel will occur, but it must be at the end of the Tribulation since the invading army will be the army of the Mahdi (the Antichrist) and will be destroyed by God. Thus, he must equate the battle of Gog & Magog in Ezekiel 38 and 39 with the Battle of Armageddon. But these are not the same battles.

The battle of Gog & Magog involves Russia and certain specified allies who come against Israel either at the beginning of the Tribulation or, most likely, before it begins. One of the tip-offs as to the timing of this invasion is the statement that following the defeat of the invading armies, the Jews will spend seven years burning the leftover weapons (Ezekiel 39: 9).

Many have equated this seven years with the Tribulation, thus putting the invasion at the start of that period of time. But we know that in the middle of the Tribulation the Antichrist is going to turn on the Jews and try to annihilate them, causing them to flee the nation (Revelation 12:13-17). This will make it impossible for them to continue the burning of weapons during the last half of that terrible period. So, most likely, the battle will occur before the Tribulation begins.

In contrast, the Battle of Armageddon occurs at the end of the Tribulation. And there really is no battle at all. The armies of the Antichrist are destroyed in an instant when Jesus returns to the Mount of Olives and speaks a supernatural word, causing their flesh to drop from their bodies (Zechariah 14:1-13). In the Gog & Magog battle, the invading armies will be destroyed on the "mountains of Israel" (Ezekiel 39:4), not in the Valley of Armageddon, and they will be destroyed by pestilence, hailstones, fire and brimstone (Ezekiel 38:22).

Another difference can be found in the motivation of the wars. The War of Gog & Magog results from God "putting hooks in the jaws" of the invading nations and dragging them down against Israel "to capture spoil and to seize plunder" (Ezekiel 38:4 & 12). In contrast, the armies of the world that will be assembled at Armageddon will be gathered by demon spirits (Revelation 16:13-16).

Another serious problem with placing the Gog & Magog war at the end of the Tribulation is that Ezekiel 38 says the invasion will occur at a time when Israel is living in peace with unwalled cities (Ezekiel 38:11). That will not be the case at the end of the Tribulation. The land of Israel will be in absolute chaos at that time.

A Final Argument

Richardson wraps up his arguments with the observation that the Antichrist must be a Muslim because Islam is the most perfect incarnation of the antichrist spirit.[36] He makes this assertion because Islam denies the Trinity, rejects Jesus as the Son of God, and repudiates the crucifixion of Jesus, arguing that someone else was killed in His place.

I do not agree with this observation. To me, the most perfect incarnation of the antichrist spirit is, and always has been, Humanism in all its various forms. Islam points people toward a god, even though he is a false god. Humanism encourages people to worship Man. God is denied. Man is exalted. And I believe the rejection of God, together with the exaltation of self, is the ultimate antichrist spirit.

Anticipating Objections

Richardson concludes his book by dealing with what he calls "potential problems with his thesis." He mentions only two.

The first is the fact that the Bible states that in the middle of the Tribulation, when the Antichrist goes to Jerusalem and desecrates the Temple, he will declare himself to be God (2 Thessalonians 2:4). Richardson says this is possibly the strongest argument that can be made against his thesis since it is inconceivable that any Muslim would ever claim to be God. Nonetheless, he argues that the Muslim Antichrist will become so self-absorbed that he will do so, and he claims that when it happens, the Muslims will be too embarrassed to confess that they have been deceived![37]

I'm sorry, but I find this very hard to believe. To me, that is like saying that the Muslims would be willing to agree that night is day and day is night. There is a limit to deception. A person would have to cease being a Muslim in order to believe that any man could be God.

I believe the bizarre behavior of the Antichrist described in 2 Thessalonians 2:3-4, where it states that he will proclaim himself to be God, rules out any possibility that the Antichrist might prove to be a Muslim.

An equally important fact that I think rules out the possibility of a Muslim Antichrist is that prophecy states the Antichrist will make a covenant with Israel that will guarantee the nation's security (Daniel 9:27 and Isaiah 28:14-22). I think it is preposterous to believe that Israel would ever trust its security to a Muslim leader or that a Muslim leader would be interested in guaranteeing the safety of Israel.

The second problem Richardson anticipates relates to his scrambling of the Islamic order of end time events by placing the appearance of the Islamic Dajjal at the end of the Tribulation instead of at the beginning. Incredibly, he says that the Muslims will simply overlook this problem due to the inconsistency of Hadith traditions. As he puts it, once the Mahdi has conquered Israel and taken Jerusalem, the Muslims will accept him regardless of the fact that the Dajjal was supposed to come first.[38]

But again, this overlooks the fact that according to biblical prophecy, the first thing the Antichrist will do is make a peace treaty with Israel, not defeat Israel. And I would contend that any Muslim leader who would make peace with Israel would be rejected by the Muslim world, just as was the case with Anwar Sadat, the President of Egypt, when he signed a peace treaty with Israel. He was assassinated by Islamic fundamentalists almost immediately.

There are other serious problems with Richardson's scenario that he does not acknowledge. How, for example, does he explain the miraculous resurrection of the Roman Empire in the form of the European Union? It's a development that prophecy experts have been telling us to watch for, and those alerts go back several hundred years. Is the revival of the Roman Empire just an accident of history? I think not. I believe that, just as the Bible prophesies, it is going to serve as the platform for the ascension of the Antichrist.

Another problem Richardson must deal with is the worldwide destruction that Revelation describes in chapters 6-9. Those chapters reveal that one-half of the world's population is going to die during the first half of the Tribulation. Is this going to happen as a result of a regional conflict? Or, is all this just more "biblical hyperbole"?

Two Questions

When I finished reading Richardson's book, I found myself wanting to ask him two questions. The first was what is he going to do with Psalm 83?[39] This psalm portrays an attack on Israel by a Muslim coalition consisting of Jordan, Egypt, Lebanon, Gaza, Saudi Arabia and Assyria (Syria). The Bible clearly teaches that God will protect Israel against all such attacks in the end times (Zechariah 12:6).

The outcome of this war most likely is detailed in Zephaniah 2:4-5. These verses indicate that the attacking nations will be devastated by Israel. It is during this war that Damascus, the capital of Syria, will probably be destroyed completely, never to be rebuilt again (Isaiah 17:1-14 and Jeremiah 49:23-27). That is most likely why Syria is not mentioned in Ezekiel 38 as one of the Russian allies.

The outcome of the Psalm 83 war is what will most likely produce peace for Israel, the peace that it is prophesied to be enjoying when Russia and its allies decide to launch the Ezekiel 38 invasion.

The war of Psalm 83 followed by the war of Ezekiel 38 will result in the annihilation of nearly all the armies of the Muslim nations of the Middle East, and these wars are most likely going to occur before the Tribulation begins! Thus, if the Antichrist is a Muslim who is going to rule a Muslim empire in the Middle East during the Tribulation, then he is going to rule over an empire that has been reduced to ashes!

The second question Richardson left hanging relates to the timing of the Rapture. He never mentions the event, leaving the clear impression that he identifies it with the Second Coming of Jesus.

Shoebat's Book

The book published in 2008 by Walid Shoebat with the aid of Joel Richardson, adds very little to the debate, but it does clarify some issues.

With regard to the Rapture, Shoebat dismisses it out of hand as being of no importance. Specifically, he writes: "Whether the Rapture is a Pre-Tribulation, Mid, or Post-Tribulation event is irrelevant . . ." He then adds, "I do daily pray for a Pre-Tribulation Rapture, and always prepare for a Post. I am of neither position."[40]

Regarding the timing of the war of Gog & Magog in Ezekiel 38 and 39, he confirms that he and Richardson believe it will occur at the end of the Tribulation and that it is, in fact, the same as the Battle of Armageddon.[41]

The meaning of Psalm 83 is specifically addressed.[42] Shoebat attempts to prove that the war described in this psalm between Israel and its adjacent Arab neighbors is one that will occur at the end of the Tribulation, after the Second Coming of the Messiah. In other words it will be a part of the Armageddon Campaign that will include the Battle of Gog & Magog. Thus, he argues it will be a conflict between forces led by Jesus and those led by the Mahdi. I was astonished to read this interpretation because I have studied this psalm in detail, and there is not one verse in it that even implies that Jesus will be present on this earth when the battle occurs.

So, I looked for Shoebat's scriptural proof of Jesus' presence. Believe it or not, the proof he provided was quotes from two other psalms:

1) Psalm 82:8 — "Arise, O God, judge the earth!"

2) Psalm 80:14 — "Return, we beseech You, O God of hosts."

Neither one of the psalms are related to Psalm 83. Both are prayers by Asaph for the Lord to return to the earth to bring justice. Neither one states that the Messiah is on the earth.

This kind of incredibly sloppy proof-texting can be found throughout Shoebat's book. Whenever he wants to make a point, he goes fishing for a verse. When he finds it, he reels it in and applies it to the issue under consideration, whether it is related to that issue or not.

Another example can be found in the second argument he gives for placing the Psalm 83 war at the end of the Tribulation. He says it must occur at that time because it is a war triggered by the Antichrist's desecration of the Jewish Temple — a temple that will be rebuilt during the first half of the Tribulation. And what is his evidence? He quotes Psalm 79:1 — "O God, the nations have invaded Your inheritance; they have defiled Your holy temple."[43] Once again, he tries to prove a point about Psalm 83 by quoting a verse from an unrelated psalm that is most likely describing the destruction of Solomon's Temple.

Strained Logic

Shoebat displays some tortuous logic throughout his book. A good example can be found in his attempt to explain away the meaning of Daniel 9:26, a passage Richardson avoided dealing with in his book. The plain sense meaning of this passage is that the Antichrist will come from the people who will destroy the Temple.

Shoebat tries to dispel this meaning by arguing that the Roman legions that carried out the destruction of Jerusalem and the Temple in 70 AD were composed primarily of Syrians and Turks. He therefore concludes that the Antichrist will arise from the Syrians or Turks and will be a Muslim.[44]

But Shoebat's argument here is really grasping at straws in the wind! The ethnicity of the soldiers is irrelevant. It would not have made any difference if the legions had been composed of Australian Aborigines, for it was the Roman government that decided to destroy Jerusalem, it was the Roman government that gave the orders, and it was Roman generals who carried out the destruction. Rome was the rod of God's judgment and it is from the Roman people that the Antichrist will arise.

Strange Points

At times Shoebat gets absolutely weird. For example, he says that one day while he was examining the Codex Vaticanus Greek text of the Book of Revelation, he noticed "that the supposed Greek letters (Chi Xi Sigma) that are used to translate to the number 666 very much resemble the most common creed of Islam . . . written in Arabic."[45]

The lower case Greek letters for Chi Xi Sigma are as follows: χ ξ ς

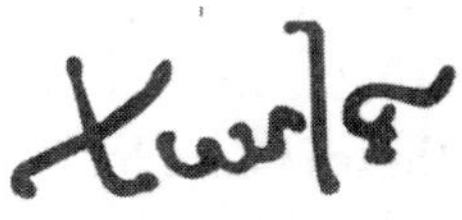

The condensed Islamic creed, shown to the right, literally means (reading right to left): "In the Name of Allah," followed by the symbol of crossed swords.

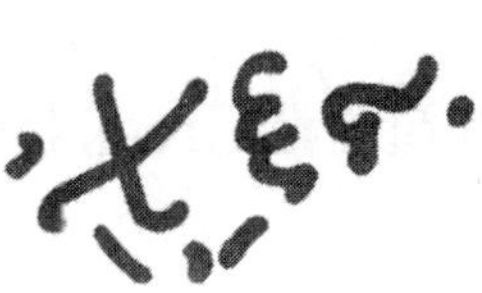

He then observes that the Greek text for 666 (shown to the right) looks like the Islamic creed except that the word, "Allah," is presented vertically, with the crossed swords to the left of it.

He then asks, "Is it possible that the Apostle John, while receiving his divine revelation, did not see Greek letters, but instead was supernaturally shown Arabic words and an Islamic symbol, which he then faithfully recorded?"[46]

The answer, of course, is no! The reason I can be so emphatic about it is because the verse (Revelation 13:18) says three times that it is talking about a number.

A Recent Revision

In 2010 Joel Richardson came out with a new explanation of Daniel 9:26, undoubtedly in response to the withering criticism that the previous explanation had received.[47]

He begins his new interpretation by pointing out that the destruction of Jerusalem by Titus in 70 AD did not fall within the first 483 years of Daniel's 490 year prophecy. Rather, it occurred 40 years after the close of that period. Thus, he surmises that the prophecy concerning the Temple's destruction most likely points to the last seven years of Daniel's prophecy — the period of the Tribulation when he believes the Temple will be destroyed by the Mahdi.

He admits that the Scriptures do not specifically state that the Temple will be destroyed during the Tribulation, but he says the destruction is implied in Revelation 11:1-2 where it states that the Gentiles "will trample on the holy city for 42 months." He also points to Luke 21:20 where it is stated that Jerusalem will experience "desolation," but that verse clearly applies to the destruction of the Temple in 70 AD.[48]

So Richardson has gone from completely ignoring Daniel 9:26 to arguing that it was not the Romans who destroyed the Temple in 70 AD to now stating that the prophecy probably relates to a future destruction that is yet to occur during the Tribulation.

I think what we have here is a perfect illustration of a desperate attempt to manipulate both Bible prophecy and Islamic prophecy to conform to a pre-conceived end time scenario.

Even a cursory look at Daniel 9:26 reveals that the destruction of the Temple that it prophesies, occurs *after* the Messiah has been "cut off," that is, after the end of the first 483 years and *before* the beginning of the final Tribulation period of seven years.

The European Union

Another recent article by Richardson gloats over internal problems being experienced by the European Union. It was titled "EU Collapse: Doom for popular Bible prophecies?"[49] Richardson observed: "Many staunch adherents to the Euro-centered end time theory are slowly awakening to the possibility that soon there may not even be a European Union at all." He goes so far as to compare the prediction of an end time revival of the Roman Empire to the Watchtower's proclamation that Jesus would return in 1975! I found this comparison to be downright ludicrous, considering the fact that Jesus did not return in 1975 but the Roman Empire has been revived, as predicted, in the form of the European Union.

Further, I found this attack to be amusing, because I consider the internal problems of the European Union to be a fulfillment of Bible prophecy. After all, what was the symbol of the revived Roman Empire in Nebuchadnezzar's dream? It was the feet mixed of iron and clay. Such a mixture is inherently unstable, and I have always interpreted it to mean that the revived Roman Empire of the end times would be a loose confederation of states before being galvanized into a powerful empire by the Antichrist.

Muslim Triumph or Defeat?

Rather than a great Muslim triumph under the leadership of a Muslim Antichrist, I believe the most likely end time scenario for the Muslim world will be one of overwhelming defeat, first in the regional wars of Psalm 83 and Ezekiel 38 and then in the world wars of Revelation 6, 8 and 9. Muslim power in the Middle East will be dealt a terrible blow in the wars of Psalm 83 and Ezekiel 38, both of which I think will most likely occur before the beginning of the Tribulation.

But the biggest portion of the Muslim world lives outside the Middle East. The largest Muslim nations today are Indonesia, Pakistan, India, and Bangladesh. It is these nations that I believe will offer the strongest resistance to the European Antichrist, and I believe they will be destroyed in the world war the Antichrist will launch, a war that begins as a conventional one in Revelation 6 but which appears to eventually morph into a nuclear one in Revelation 8 and 9, resulting in the destruction of one half of the earth's population.

Concluding Thoughts

Overall, I think what Richardson and Shoebat are presenting as a possible end time scenario of events is a hodgepodge of ideas drawn from Bible prophecy, Islamic prophecy, and their own rich imaginations. What they present is not true to either Bible prophecy or Islamic prophecy.

Two final observations. First, beware of Lone Ranger interpretations of prophecy that are not widely shared. God does not reveal the meaning of prophecy only to a person or two. Second Peter 1:20 says, "no prophecy of Scripture is a matter of one's own interpretation." Private and peculiar interpretations, like the recent "Pre-Wrath Rapture," usually make a big initial splash and then fade quickly when submitted to critical review.

Second, I think the current rush to identify the Antichrist as a Muslim is a classic example of newspaper exegesis — of reading the news headlines into the Bible rather than letting the Bible speak for itself. It would be good to keep in mind a comment made by the great Bible teacher Ray Stedman: "What determines the future is what God has done in the past and what He has promised to do in the future. So don't look horizontally at current events."[50]

THE NAMING OF THE ANTICHRIST

"Let no one in any way deceive you, for it [the day of the Lord] will not come unless the apostasy comes first, and the man of lawlessness is revealed, the son of destruction."—
2 Thessalonians 2:3

Trying to identify the Antichrist by name is an intellectual sport played by Bible prophecy fanatics and sensationalists. In my opinion, it ranks in irresponsibility right up there with attempts to establish the date of the Lord's return.

The Bible makes it clear that we cannot know the identity of the Antichrist before the day of the Lord, which begins with the onset of the Tribulation (2 Thessalonians 2:1-3). It also clearly states that no one can know the date of the Lord's return for His Church (Matthew 24:36).

Exercises in Silliness

Back in the 1990's I had a colleague named Dennis Pollock who assisted me with a radio program we were producing at the time. It was called "Christ in Prophecy." Dennis became outraged over the attempts that were being made to identify the Antichrist. He came to me one day and asked if he could do a whole program about how ridiculous it is to try to identify the Antichrist. I agreed to his idea.

Now, Dennis is a fellow with a great sense of humor, and he knows how to use it very effectively to make a point. Accordingly, he began the radio program in a satirical way by asserting that a popular kid's TV hero at the time, Barney the

Purple Dinosaur was the Antichrist!

He then proceeded to try to prove his point in the following manner:

1) Start with the name.
   CUTE PURPLE DINOSAUR

2) Change all U's to V's (as in Latin).
   CVTE PVRPLE DINOSAVR

3) Extract all Roman numerals.
   C V V L D I V

4) Convert to Arabic values.
   100/5/5/50/500/1/5

5) Add all the numbers, and they total 666!

Thus, since Barney's name adds up to 666, Barney must be the Antichrist!

A couple of days later we received an irate letter from a man who had tuned in late to the program and concluded that Dennis was seriously trying to prove that Barney was the Antichrist! Some people just don't have a sense of humor.

The sad thing about this story is that it is very illustrative of many of the serious attempts that have been made to identify the Antichrist.

For example, shortly after the election of Barack Obama, prophecy teacher Don McGee received a letter in which the author tried to prove that the new president was the Antichrist. He arbitrarily assigned numerical values to each letter of the English alphabet and then start calculating the value of various phrases:

Barack Obama Mark	= 666
Barack Obama Planned	= 666
The Fierce Obama	= 666

Democrat Obama	= 666
Obama Wound	= 666
Obama and Dragon	= 666

Of course all these calculations ignored two facts: 1) There are no recognized numerical values for letters in the English alphabet, and 2) The 666 referred to in Revelation 13:18 is supposed to be the value of the Antichrist's name, not his name plus a title or his name plus a modifier.

An equally silly attempt to identify President Obama as the Antichrist appeared in 2009 in the form of a brief video on YouTube that went viral. A Christian pastor posted the video which was titled, "Did Jesus actually reveal the name of the Antichrist ?"[1]

The thesis of the video was based on a statement of Jesus recorded in Luke 10:18 — "I beheld Satan as lightning fall from heaven" (KJV). The pastor, who identified himself only as "ppsimmons," said that he started doing research on the statement and discovered that the Greek word for lightning is *astrape*, and that the Hebrew equivalent is *baraq*. When he looked up the Greek word for heaven, he discovered that it can refer to "high places" or "heights," as well as the heaven where God dwells. That reminded him of Isaiah 14:14 where Lucifer — another name for Satan — is quoted saying, "I will ascend above the heights of the clouds; I will be like the most High." And, lo and behold, when he looked up the Hebrew word, heights, it was *bamah*.

Thus, the video concludes with the observation that "if spoken by a Jewish rabbi today, influenced by the poetry of Isaiah, he would say these words in Hebrew: 'I saw Satan as Baraq Ubamah.'"

Talk about a stretch! He goes from English to Greek to Hebrew and then back to an English wording that ignores the construction of the original sentence. It is an exercise in silliness. Yet millions were enthralled by it.

The Key Scripture Passage

Speculation about the identity of the Antichrist is based on Revelation 13:16-18 where it states that during the Great Tribulation people will have to take a mark on their right hand or forehead in order to buy or sell anything. The mark will be either the name of the beast (the Antichrist) or the number of his name — and that number will be 666.

The concept of a number for the name of the Antichrist is a reference to what is called gematria, which is a system whereby a numerical number is assigned to each letter of the alphabet. Such a system existed in biblical times for both Hebrew and Greek. It has never existed in English because Arabic numerals have always been used in English.[2]

A good example of gematria is to be found in the Hebrew word, *chai*, which means life. The word in Hebrew is composed of two letters that add up to 18. This has made 18 a "lucky number" among Jews.

Now, since the name of the Antichrist will add up to 666, people are constantly trying to find a world leader, past or present whose name adds up to that number. Dead people are candidates because some interpret Revelation 13 to teach that the Antichrist will be resurrected from the dead.

So, calculations are always being made, some in Hebrew, some in Greek, and some in English. But the New Testament was written in Greek to a Greek speaking audience, and therefore it is pretty clear that only the values of Greek letters should be used. Translating from Greek to Hebrew, and then using the values assigned to Hebrew letters cannot be valid. And the English language has no accepted numerical values for the letters of its alphabet — so exercises in English are also futile. Realizing this, some have tried to get around the problem in novel ways. For example, there were those who claimed Ronald Reagan was the Antichrist because his full name, Ronald Wilson Reagan, had 6 letters in each name, resulting in 666!

Nero as a Candidate

Preterist theologians typically support the idea that the numerical interpretation of 666 is the Roman Emperor Nero who reigned from 54 to 68 AD.[3]

Preterists are those who believe that the book of Revelation was written before 70 AD and that most, if not all, of the prophecies in the book were fulfilled in the destruction of Jerusalem, including, for some, the Second Coming of Jesus. Therefore, they are compelled to argue that the Antichrist has already appeared in history — and their candidate is Nero.

But there is a major problem with identifying Nero as the Antichrist. His name in Greek adds up to 1,005. So what the Preterists have done is add the title of Caesar to his name and then translate the phrase, Nero Caesar, from Greek to Hebrew, coming up with a numerical value of 666. In short, they have resorted to a lot of manipulation in order to achieve their goal.

Nero Caesar was not Nero's name. That's his name plus a title. Nero did not rule over all the world as the Bible says the Antichrist will do (Revelation 13:8). There is no record in Roman history of a person who corresponds to the second beast of Revelation 13 — the False Prophet. Finally, the book of Revelation states that the Antichrist will reign for 7 years. Nero reigned for 14 years.

Beyond the Preterists there are people who believe that Nero will be resurrected in the end times to serve as the Antichrist. One of those is Gary Bowers who is the author of a book titled, *Out of the Abyss*.[4]

Bowers bases his entire thesis on a statement in Revelation 17:8 which reads: "The beast you [the Apostle John] saw was and is not, and is about to come up out of the abyss and go to destruction . . ." The beast that is referred to here is the one pictured in verse 3 that a woman is riding.

According to Bowers, this verse convinced him that the Antichrist had to have been alive before John saw it, that it was no longer alive, but that one day it would be alive again. But this assumption on the part of Bowers is not valid. John is being given a vision about events that will take place in the future, not about things that had already taken place. John is being told that in the end times, a corrupt religious system (represented by the woman) will be used by the Antichrist to consolidate his world empire until it becomes a nuisance to him, at which point he will destroy it (verse 16).

The reference to the beast who "was and is not, and is about to come up" is simply speaking of the future Antichrist who will suffer a wound "as if it had been slain" and then will be healed (Revelation 13:3). An alternative interpretation is that it is speaking of the revival of the Roman Empire in the end times out of which the Antichrist will come.

Bower's next step is to try to identify the person referred to as having lived, is now dead, but will be resurrected. For that identification, he points to Revelation 17:9-11 which says that the seven heads of the beast on which the woman is sitting represent seven kings, "five of which have fallen, one is, the other has not yet come," These are usually interpreted to be the seven great Gentile empires of Bible prophecy. The five fallen would be Egypt, Assyria, Babylon, Medo-Persia, and Greece. The "one that is" would be the one that existed at that time, namely Rome. And "the one to come" would be the end time revival of the Roman Empire. The passage also refers to an eighth kingdom — the last Gentile kingdom — and identifies it as the kingdom of the beast (the Antichrist), saying it will be one of the seven, meaning it comes out of the revival of the Roman Empire.

But Bowers insists that these passages are not speaking of kingdoms past and future but of kings who lived at the time John wrote the book of Revelation. He concludes, therefore, that the Antichrist must come from among the Roman emperors who reigned before John wrote the book.

The problem is that there were 12 of them from Augustus (27 BC-14 AD) to Nerva (96-98 AD), and the passage in Revelation speaks of only 7 — "five have fallen, one is, the other is yet to come" (Revelation 17:10). In order to whittle the list down to 7, Bowers starts playing games with the list of names. He tries to argue that the word, fallen, refers only to the ones who were killed, as opposed to those who died a natural death. He then points out that 5 of the Emperors were killed. Those would be the "five fallen." The "one is" would be the Emperor ruling when John wrote the book of Revelation — Domitian. The one "yet to come" would be Nerva who succeeded Domitian.

According to Revelation 17:11, there will be an eighth king who is "one of the seven." This has always been interpreted to mean that the last Gentile kingdom, the kingdom of the Antichrist, will come out of a revival of the old Roman Empire. But Bowers says no, it is a reference to the Antichrist being one of the five kings who were killed — Caligula, Claudius, Nero, Galba or Vitellius.

So, which is it? He selects Nero because his name and title in Hebrew add up to 666.

Incredibly, Bowers tries to buttress this conclusion by reference to 2 Thessalonians 2:1-8 where Paul characterizes the Antichrist as "the man of lawlessness" and states that he cannot be revealed until the one restraining him is taken out of the way.[5] Paul is, of course, speaking here of the end times and the removal of the restraining influence of the Church when the Rapture takes place. But Bowers argues that the prophecy was partially fulfilled in Paul's time!

Bowers denies that the restrainer in this passage is the Holy Spirit, or the Church, or human government. Instead, he argues it was the Emperor Claudius, and with his death, the Antichrist, Nero, was revealed. In the end times, after Nero is resurrected, he will fulfill the rest of Paul's prophecy when he enters the rebuilt Temple in Jerusalem and declares himself to be God.

All I can say is welcome to the weird world and convoluted reasoning of those who are determined to identify the Antichrist!

Augustus as a Candidate

A similar line of argument is pursued by John Claeys in his book, *Apocalypse 2012*.[6]

Although he is not a Preterist, Claeys argues that the book of Revelation was written in 68 AD, before the Roman destruction of Jerusalem. This, of course, flies in the face of all the internal and historical evidence that clearly establishes the authorship of Revelation in 95 AD.[7]

Again, like Gary Bowers, Claeys focuses on Revelation 17:10, asserting that it is speaking about specific kings and not kingdoms. And since the passage refers to five kings who have already fallen, that means that John must have been writing during the reign of the sixth emperor, Galba, who ruled from 68-69 AD. The sixth king, the one 'not yet come," would be Galba's successor, Emperor Otho. And since the eighth king mentioned is the Antichrist — referred to as "one of the seven," Claeys concludes that he will be one of the first seven emperors, resurrected from the dead.

As to which one, Claeys choice is the first Roman emperor, Augustus. Why him? Because "he was the architect of the Roman Empire, and he was an administrative genius."[8]

The only saving grace is that Claeys does not get engaged in mathematical gymnastics in an attempt to prove that the name of Augustus adds up to 666. But that's because he dismisses the number as being probably nothing more than the Antichrist's registration number in the new world order![9]

Prince Charles as a Candidate

In a book titled, *The Antichrist and a Cup of Tea*, the author, Tim Cohen, presents Prince Charles of England as the perfect candidate for the Antichrist.[10] I met the author at a prophecy conference in Denver several years ago, and when he told me his thesis, I thought he was kidding. I laughed and said, "If that wimp, Prince Charles, is the Antichrist, then Satan is in big trouble!" The author then assured me that he was serious about his contention, and he observed that the looks and behavior of Prince Charles are part of a charade to shield his true identity. "When the time comes for him to be revealed as the Antichrist," said Cohen, "it will be like Clark Kent going into a phone booth and emerging as Superman!"

I think it is interesting to note that in the preface of the book, Cohen says that he got the original idea from a Messianic Jew in Oklahoma by the name of Monte Judah, a Bible teacher who happens to be a proven false prophet.[11] Cohen took the idea and ran with it, producing a book 444 pages long.

Cohen begins with 666, arguing that the name and title, Prince Charles of Wales, adds up to 666 in both Hebrew and English.[12] There are two problems here. First, the relevant passage in the Bible — Revelation 13:16-18 — was written in Greek, not Hebrew. Second, as I have already pointed out several times, the letters in the English alphabet have no assigned numbers because Arabic numerals are used in English.

Recognizing these problems, Cohen makes an astounding declaration: "In the author's opinion, the weight of the evidence presented herein regarding Prince Charles is so great that even if there were no known numbering system whereby his name calculated to 666, one would nonetheless be compelled to conclude that he is plausibly the Antichrist."[13] Translation: "I don't care what the Bible says about his name adding up to 666 because the evidence I am going to present is overwhelming." Incredible!

Cohen then proceeds to present his "evidence:"

1) Prince Charles is not only of Roman heritage, as the Antichrist must be, but he can claim descent from King David and may actually be a member of the tribe of Dan from which many believe the Antichrist will come.

2) His heritage gives him a right to claim the Crusader title of King of Jerusalem.

3) His heraldic coat of arms "is a literal, graphic representation of the beast described in Daniel and in the Apocalypse."

4) He is respected worldwide and "is extremely well connected — royally, religiously, environmentally, militarily, financially, and otherwise."

5) While he is viewed as a Christian, he is "thoroughly anti-Christian, coming from a family with a long history of involvement in Satanism and the occult."

Prince Hassan as a Candidate

In 2007 Joe VanKoevering attempted to identify the Antichrist in a book titled, *Unveiling the Man of Sin*.[14] VanKoevering begins his quest for the Antichrist by claiming that he must be of Assyrian heritage. His biblical basis for this assertion is Isaiah 10:24 — "Therefore, thus says the Lord

God of hosts, 'O My people who dwell in Zion, do not fear the Assyrian who strikes you with the rod and lifts up his staff against you, the way Egypt did.'"

Next, he resorts to the argument that since Antiochus Epiphanes — a type of the Antichrist — came from the Seleucid or Assyrian area of the Grecian Empire (Syria and Iraq), the Antichrist must also come from that area.

He then tries to narrow down the search to one modern day country within the old Assyrian Empire. He does this by pointing out that in Daniel 11 there is a description of the Antichrist's invasion of the Middle East during the Tribulation. Daniel says the Antichrist and his army will conquer Israel and Egypt but will not enter the area of modern day Jordan. This prompts VanKoevering to conclude that the Antichrist will come from Jordan.

In response, I would point out first of all that Isaiah 10:24 has absolutely nothing to do with end time prophecy. Isaiah 10 is a prophecy that God will use Assyria as His "rod of anger" (verse 5) to judge Israel. He urges Israel in verses 24-25 not to fear the Assyrians because "in a very little while My indignation against you will be spent, and My anger will be directed to their destruction." In other words, God will use Assyria to discipline Israel but He will not allow them to destroy the Jewish people. And furthermore, once He is finished using Assyria as a rod of His discipline, He will destroy the Assyrian Empire.

That's all there is to the passage. Again, it has nothing to do with end time prophecy or the Antichrist.

With regard to Antiochus Epiphanes being a prophetic type of the Antichrist, the Bible presents many other such types, including the Pharaoh of the Exodus and King Saul of Israel, but these types do not mean the Antichrist will necessarily come from Egypt or Israel. But the most important fact to keep in mind is that Antiochus was a Greek, not an Assyrian.

As to the argument based on Daniel 11, it is true that the Antichrist and his armies will not enter modern day Jordan. But the reason given is that the area will be "rescued out of his hands" (Daniel 11:41). That doesn't sound like a voluntary decision to refrain from invading the area. Rather, it sounds like God prevents the Antichrist from invading Jordan — and for good reason, since the Bible indicates this will be the land of refuge for the Jewish remnant when they flee Israel in the middle of the Tribulation (Revelation 12:13-17).

Besides asserting that the Antichrist must be an Assyrian, VanKoevering also says he must be a "prince" and "the King of Babylon."

The prince requirement is taken from Daniel 9:26 which says the Antichrist will be a prince. The King of Babylon idea comes from Isaiah 14:4ff where a taunt against the King of Babylon is presented. As the King of Babylon is described in detail, he clearly morphs into a description of Satan. VanKoevering claims it is also a description of the Antichrist.

Having established what he believes are three requirements for the Antichrist — that he be an Assyrian from Jordan, that he be a prince, and that he be the King of Babylon — VanKoevering then spends the rest of his book trying to prove that the best candidate for the Antichrist is Crown Prince El Hassan bin Talal of Jordan![15] Prince Hassan is the brother of former King Hussein and was his designated heir to the throne of Jordan until the king changed his mind on his deathbed and gave the throne, instead, to his son, Abdullah II.

Why does he point to Prince Hassan? First, he argues that "the closest genetic relationship of the Assyrians are with the native populations of Jordan and Iraq."[16] But what he overlooks is the fact that the Hashemite royal family of Jordan is not native to either Jordan or Iraq. The family came, instead, from Saudi Arabia. Members of this family were imposed upon the populations of Iraq and Jordan as kings of these nations by Great Britain after World War I. So, Prince Hassan does not even meet the first criterion stipulated by Van-Koevering!

The next qualification of the Antichrist that Hassan is supposed to fulfill is that he carries the title of prince. This is really irrelevant. When Daniel 9:26 says the Antichrist will be a "prince," all it is saying is that he will be a political leader. The Bible uses two terms for political leaders — prince and king. The biblical authors could not refer to presidents or prime ministers because those forms of ruling power had not yet developed. Thus, when we are told in Psalm 118:9 "it is better to take refuge in the Lord than to trust in princes," we are being warned against putting our trust in politicians. The warning is not limited to those politicians who literally have the title of prince.

VanKoevering's third qualification for the Antichrist — that he be the King of Babylon — is, of course, unfulfilled in the life of Prince Hassan. But VanKoevering argues it could become a possibility since one of his Hashemite relatives, King Faisal, was installed by the British as King of Iraq in 1921. King Faisal, the brother of Prince Hassan's grandfather, King Abdullah, died in 1933. His son, King Faisal II, and all his family were murdered in 1958 when the Iraqi military mounted a coup d'etat.

VanKoevering believes there is an excellent possibility that the leaders of Iraq will seek to stabilize their nation by inviting Prince Hassan to become king. But that is pure speculation, and there is no indication that the people of Iraq want a king, particularly one that is not even native to their population.

Nor is there any requirement in Scripture that the Antichrist be the King of Babylon. The passage VanKoevering uses to establish this idea is found in Isaiah 14 where the King of Babylon is presented as a type of Satan himself. That there might be a double application to both Satan and the Antichrist is a real possibility since the Antichrist will be possessed by Satan, but there is no indication in the passage that the Antichrist must be the King of Babylon.

A similar taunt is presented in Ezekiel 28 against the King of Tyre. And like the passage in Isaiah 14, the taunt morphs into a description of Satan that could be applied to the Antichrist. Does that mean the Antichrist must also be the King of Tyre? I think not.

Conclusion

All of these efforts to identify the Antichrist by name are exercises in futility. Like trying to set the date for the Lord's return, efforts to name the Antichrist give the whole field of Bible prophecy a bad reputation and cause Bible prophecy to be held in contempt as a playground for fanatics.

I think it is interesting to note that one of the Church Fathers, Irenaeus, writing in the year 189 AD warned against speculating about the identity of the Antichrist:[17]

> Moreover, another danger, by no means trifling, shall overtake those who falsely presume that they know the name of the Antichrist. For if these men assume one [name] when this [Antichrist] shall come having another, they will be easily led away by him as supposing him not to be the expected one . . . It is therefore more certain, and less hazardous, to await the fulfillment of the prophecy than to be making surmises and casting about for any names that may present themselves, inasmuch as many names can be found pos-

> sessing the number mentioned, and the same question will, after all, remain unsolved.

That's very sage advice from 1,800 years ago, and it needs to be heeded today.

In the study, teaching and preaching of Bible prophecy, we need to focus on Jesus Christ and not the Antichrist.

THE GOD OF THE ANTICHRIST

"And the dragon [Satan] gave him [the Antichrist] his power and his throne and great authority . . . And it was given to him to make war with the saints and to overcome them, and authority over every tribe and people and tongue and nation was given to him."

— Revelation 13:2,7

Planet earth is in rebellion against God and has been for 6,000 years, ever since Eve was enticed by Satan to sin. This planet was originally created for Mankind, and God granted Adam and Eve sovereignty over it (Genesis 1:28-31). But when they sinned, they lost that precious sovereignty to Satan, and he has been the god of this world ever since (2 Corinthians 4:4 and 1 John 5:19).

But Satan wants more than that. He desires to overthrow the very throne of God in Heaven and to be worshiped on earth as God by all Mankind. He has a plan for accomplishing these goals, and the Antichrist is a key element in that plan.

Satan is the one who will select the Antichrist, possess him spiritually, empower him politically, and manipulate his leadership. Satan and the Antichrist will become one when Satan possesses him, and there is no way to fully understand the Antichrist without a knowledge of who Satan is, how he operates, and what he hopes to accomplish.

So, who is this god of the Antichrist? Where did he come from? What are his characteristics? How will he interact with the Antichrist? And what will be his ultimate destiny?

Dismissing Satan

The irony of Satan is that despite his incredible power and his overwhelming influence for evil in the world, most people do not seem to take him seriously. For many he is nothing more than a cartoon character in a red suit with a sneer on his face, horns on his head, and a pitchfork in his hand.

Recent polls have revealed that 60% of Americans believe Satan is just a symbol of evil and not a living being.[1] Even 52% of Christians who identify themselves as "born-again" deny the reality of Satan.[2]

Celebrities often mock Satan and Hell. I remember a few years ago when the 70th birthday party of Willie Nelson was televised nationally. At one point they showed a collection of video tributes to the famed Country singer. One of Willie's well known friends laughed and said, "Happy birthday, Willie! I look forward to partying with you in Hell!"

Conan O'Brien, the popular late night TV host, wrote and performed a song mocking Hell. The song is so perverse that only parts can be quoted. The following section will give you the idea:[3]

> I'm gonna go to Hell when I die
> I'm gonna go to Hell when I die
>
> I can't be saved, it's too late for me
> I'm going to H-E Double L when I D-I-E
> You could say I'm messed up, but I'm keepin' it real
> I'll sleep with your mom for a home cooked meal
> Give a guy with no legs a new pair of shoes
> And give Ben Affleck a bottle of booze
> I call up Nick Lechey, tell him he's gay
> Then ask Jessica to spell Chevrolet
>
> I'm gonna go to Hell when I die

Cable television's Ted Turner mocked Hell in a similar manner when he said, "I don't need anybody to die for me. I've had a few drinks and a few girlfriends, and if that's gonna put me in Hell, then so be it."[4]

The Australian hard rock band, AC/DC, released an album in 1979 titled, Highway to Hell. The title song bragged about their determination to end up in Hell:[5]

> Ain't nothing I would rather do
> Going down, party time
> My friends are gonna be there too
> I'm on the highway to Hell
> No stop signs or speed limit
> Nobody's gonna slow me down
> Hey, Satan paid my dues
> Playing in a rocking band
> Hey, Momma, look at me
> I'm on the way to the promised land
> I'm on the highway to Hell

The heavy metal band called Acheron has an album titled, "The Rites of the Black Mass." On the album, a person from the Church of Satan actually reads the rites of the Black Mass as the group sings:[6]

> Glory to thee, Almighty Satan
> We praise thee, we bless thee
> We adore thee
> Thou art Lord
> Thou alone, O Mighty Satan

In their song, "The Prince," the group named Metallica sings:[7]

> Angel from below
> I wish to sell my soul
> Devil take my soul
> With diamonds you repay

I don't care for Heaven
So don't you look for me to cry
And I will burn in Hell
From the day I die

There are many other such examples of Satanic songs being peddled today by various musical groups. Most of these songs are probably parodies designed to do nothing but shock. But some of the groups profess to be Satan worshipers.

At the 1991 MTV Awards, the spokesman for the group called Red Hot Chili Peppers acknowledged the receipt of their award by announcing, "First of all, we want to thank Satan . . ."[8]

Whether the music is a parody or is a sincere expression of worship, the Satan and the Hell it glorifies do not exist. The true Satan has no interest in blessing anyone, except for the purpose of ensnaring their souls, and there will be no partying in Hell. The Word of God teaches that Satan is a real person who is interested only in the destruction of people — all people, even those who claim to worship and adore him.

Satan's Origin

Satan is a spirit being who was created by God before the creation of the heavens and the earth (Job 38:4-7). He is in no way equal to God. He is not omnipresent. He is not omniscient.

Many believe he was one of three archangels (the other two being Michael and Gabriel), but the Bible identifies only one archangel by name — Michael (Jude 9). However, the book of Daniel indicates that there may be other archangels when it says that Michael was "one of the chief princes," obviously implying there are other angels of his type (Daniel 10:13).

We are specifically told that Satan was "an anointed cherub" who was responsible for covering or guarding the throne of God (Ezekiel 28:14). In the Scriptures, cherubim appear to be angels of a higher order who are assigned special guard duties by God. The first mention of them can be found in Genesis 3:24 where we are told that after the expulsion of Adam and Eve from the Garden of Eden, God stationed cherubim on the East of Eden to prevent them from having access to the tree of life (Genesis 3:24).

Some have concluded that one of Satan's main responsibilities may have been that of a worship leader. That's because there is a reference in Ezekiel 28:13 to his "tambourines and flutes." However, the words here in Hebrew are uncertain. The King James Version refers to "tabrets and pipes." The New International Version translates the words as "settings and mountings." The New American Standard Bible refers to "settings and sockets," but provides the alternative translation of tambourines and flutes.

More definitely we are told in the Scriptures that Satan was created in perfection, and that therefore he was "full of wisdom" and "perfect in beauty" (Ezekiel 28:12-13). We are also told that he was covered with precious gems (Ezekiel 28:13).

Satan's Fall

As with all of God's higher beings, both men and angels, Satan was given free will because God desires true fellowship and not the orchestrated adoration of robots. We are told that, tragically, Satan used his free will to make a decision to rebel against God. Isaiah describes it in this way, quoting Satan (Isaiah 14:13-14):

> I will ascend to heaven;
> I will raise my throne about the stars of God,
> And I will sit on the mount of assembly . . .
> I will ascend above the heights of the clouds;

I will make myself like the Most High.

Notice the repetition of the phrase, "I will." The words literally seethe with rebellion. And Ezekiel tells us that the rebellion was rooted in pride: "Your heart was lifted up because of your beauty; you corrupted your wisdom by reason of your splendor" (Ezekiel 28:17). Satan became filled with pride, unrighteousness and violence, and his sin resulted in God casting him out of Heaven (Ezekiel 28:15-17).

When was Satan kicked out of Heaven? We can only guess. The book of Job tells us that all the angelic host (which would include Satan) "shouted with joy" when God laid the foundation of the earth (Job 38:4-7). So Satan's fall must have taken place between the time the creation was finished and Adam and Eve were tempted. At the end of the creation week, God pronounced all of His creative work to be "very good" (Genesis 1:31), so the fall of Satan had to take place after that.

The gap between the end of the creation week and the temptation of Adam and Eve could have been anywhere between a few days or a few years. We know there was a lapse of time because Adam gave names to each of God's creatures before the temptation of Eve occurred (Genesis 2:19-20).

When Satan was cast out of Heaven, he took one-third of the heavenly host with him (Revelation 12:4). Jesus referred to this event when He told His disciples, "I saw Satan fall from Heaven like lightning" (Luke 10:18). The angels who rebelled with Satan became the demonic spirits that infest our planet today. This is the reason that Satan was referred to by the Pharisees as "the ruler of the demons" (Matthew 9:34).

Satan's Reality

I want to emphasize again that Satan is not some inanimate evil force or power. He is a real person with all the traits of personality — feelings, emotions, will and intelligence.

He appeared to Jesus and tempted Him mightily in the Judean wilderness (Matthew 4:1-10). Jesus carried on a vigorous conversation with Satan. Jesus was not talking to a shadow or to Himself. Satan is never presented anywhere in the Scriptures as anything other than a supernatural spirit being — a person in every sense of the term.

Satan's Character

The character of Satan is thoroughly despicable. He is the essence of evil. He is described in the Scriptures as "a murderer" and "the father of lies" (John 8:44). The New International Version puts it colorfully when it says that when Satan lies, "he speaks his native language" (John 8:44).

Satan's basic nature is perhaps best summarized in some of the names that are given him in the Bible:

Accuser (Zechariah 3:1 and Revelation 12:10)

Adversary (Job 1:6 and 1 Peter 5:8)
This is the Hebrew meaning of Satan.

Beelzebub (Matthew 12:24, 27)
Meaning either "Lord of the flies" or "Lord of dung."

Belial (2 Corinthians 6:15)
Meaning worthless or hopeless ruin.

Deceiver (Revelation 12:9)

Destroyer (Revelation 9:11)
Apollyon in Greek or Abaddon in Hebrew.

Devil (1 John 3:8)
From the Greek word, diabolos, which means slanderer or defamer.

Dragon (Revelation 12:3-17)

Enemy (Matthew 13:39)

Evil One (John 17:15)

God of This World (2 Corinthians 4:4)

Prince of This World (John 12:31)

Roaring Lion (1 Peter 5:8)

Ruler of Darkness (Ephesians 6:12)

Serpent (Genesis 3:1 and Revelation 12:9)

Tempter (Matthew 4:3)

Thief (John 10:10)

Wicked One (Ephesians 6:16)

Satan's Domain

Two of the titles in this list are often confusing and disturbing to Christians — namely, "God of this world" and "Prince of this world." "How can this be?" people often ask. "Didn't Jesus defeat Satan at the Cross? Hasn't Satan been dethroned?"

The answer is that Satan's ultimate defeat was sealed at the Cross, but it has not yet been realized in history. That's why many years after the Cross, the Apostle John wrote, " the whole world lies in the power of the evil one" (1 John 5:19). The writer of the book of Hebrews asserts that all things have been put in subjection to Christ, "but now we do not yet see all things subjected to Him" (Hebrews 2:8).

The de-throning of Satan as the prince of this world was guaranteed by Jesus' victory over the Cross through the power of His resurrection. But Satan will not actually be removed from his throne until Jesus returns, at which time "the God of peace will crush Satan . . ." (Romans 16:20). The total defeat of Satan is a delayed benefit of the Cross, just as is the receipt of our glorified bodies.

A key aspect of the conflict between God and Satan is all about dominion. This earth was created for Mankind. God granted dominion over the creation to Adam and Eve (Genesis 1:28). But when the two of them succumbed to Satan's temptation, that dominion was lost. Satan stole it, and he became the prince of this earth. That's why he could legitimately tempt Jesus by offering Him all the kingdoms of the world if Jesus would only bow down and worship him (Matthew 4:8-10).

Satan's Freedom

Meanwhile, Satan roams about this earth like a roaring lion, seeking whom he may devour (1 Peter 5:8). This does not mean that Satan is free to do as he pleases. He is on a leash. He may be the prince of this world, but he operates under the authority of the King of the universe.

This important point is illustrated in the story of Job. Satan had to ask God's permission before he could tempt Job, and even when the permission was granted, certain limitations were placed on what Satan could do (Job 1:7-12).

This story illustrates another point. Satan currently has access to God's throne, and according to Revelation 12:10, he uses that access to accuse believers day and night.

Satan's Prophesied Fate

Satan's ultimate fate was prophesied at the very time that Adam and Eve sinned. God spoke a curse on Satan when He said:

> I will put enmity
> Between you [Satan] and the woman,
> And between your seed and her seed;
> He [the seed of woman] will bruise you on the head,
> And you shall bruise him [the seed of woman] on the heel.

This is a remarkable prophecy given at the very dawn of history. It is the first Messianic prophecy in the Bible. What God is saying here is that a person born of the seed of woman (a virgin) will suffer a wound from Satan on his heel, but he will then inflict a wound on Satan's head. The wound on the heel is symbolic of a non-lethal strike. This prophecy was fulfilled in the resurrection of Jesus from the dead. The wound on the head is symbolic of a lethal strike and will be fulfilled when Jesus returns and casts Satan into the lake of fire.

Satan's Current Activities

As we await Satan's ultimate defeat, we must deal with the temptations he and his demonic hordes place in front of us. Fortunately, those of us who are believers have the blessing of the indwelling of the Holy Spirit, and we are assured that "He who is within us is greater than he who is in the world" (1 John 4:4).

We are encouraged to "put on the full armor of God," that we might be able "to stand against the schemes of the devil" (Ephesians 6:11). And we are told that if we submit ourselves to God, then when we resist the devil, he will flee from us (James 4:7).

We are also advised to avoid giving Satan an opportunity in our lives (Ephesians 4:27). In other words, we should do everything we can to avoid temptation. And in that regard, I have learned through personal experience that it is much easier to avoid temptation than it is to resist it.

Satan's Special Man

As the signs of the end times continue to multiply, Satan must be chomping at the bit because he knows Bible prophecy (Revelation 12:12), and he realizes that the time is fast approaching when he will be able to physically manifest himself as the god of this world.

He is going to do this through a man he will anoint and then possess as his messiah (Daniel 8:24). The Bible calls this man the Antichrist (1 John 2:22), and his characteristics will be the same as Satan's. In 2 Thessalonians 2:3 he is referred to as "the son of destruction." Utilizing the power of Satan (Revelation 13:2), the Antichrist will conquer all the earth (Revelation 13:7).

And while the Antichrist is consolidating his worldwide empire, Satan will try one last time to seize the throne of God in Heaven. This will result in a heavenly war in the middle of the Tribulation. Satan and all his demons will fight against the archangel Michael and his angels. Satan will, of course, be defeated in this insane effort to displace his Creator.

We are told in Revelation that Satan will be cast down to earth and his access to Heaven will be cut off completely (Revelation 12:10-12). Satan will be filled with great wrath, and he will decide to take out his anger on the Chosen People of God — the Jews (Revelation 12:12-17).

He will begin this process by possessing the Antichrist and then motivating him to enter the rebuilt Jewish Temple in Jerusalem and declare himself to be God (2 Thessalonians 2:4), demanding that all the world worship him.

When he is rejected by the Jews, Satan will then motivate him to annihilate the Jewish people. Satan will do this because he hates the Jews with a passion. He hates them because they are God's Chosen People. He hates them because God worked through them to provide the world with the Bible. He hates them because it was through them that God sent His Son, the Messiah. And he hates them because God has promised that one day a great remnant of the Jews will turn their hearts to their Messiah and be saved (Isaiah 10:20-23, Zechariah 12:10 and Romans 9:27-28).

Satan is determined to annihilate the Jews so that God cannot fulfill His promise to bring a great remnant to salvation. Satan has tried to do this many times in the past, as with the Spanish Inquisition and the Nazi Holocaust. This will be his last attempt, and it will almost be successful, for we are told that the Antichrist will slaughter two-thirds of the Jewish people during the last half of the Tribulation (Zechariah 13:8).

Satan During the Millennium

The Tribulation will end with the Second Coming of Jesus. The Antichrist and his False Prophet will be seized and thrown alive into the lake of fire, which is Hell (Revelation 19:20-21). Satan will be seized and confined to an abyss. At that point the activity of Satan will come to a temporary end. He will be held captive for the next thousand years while Jesus reigns over all the earth from Jerusalem (Revelation 20:1-3).

At the end of the Lord's millennial reign, Satan will be set free, and he will go forth to deceive the nations (Revelation 20:7-8). This is a very perplexing development to most people. What is the purpose of releasing him?

The answer has to do with one of the fundamental purposes of the Millennium. Humanists believe that evil is rooted in society and can be uprooted through societal reforms. In sharp contrast, the Word of God teaches that evil is rooted in the fallen nature of Man (Jeremiah 17:9 and Mark 7:20-23).

God is going to disprove the Humanist theory during the Millennium. He is going to put all of Mankind into a perfect society where righteousness and justice prevail. There will be no homeless or poor people. There will be no unmet needs (Isaiah 11:4-9).

Yet, at the end of that glorious time, when Satan is released, he will rally the nations of the world against Jesus, and they will march on Jerusalem to overthrow the King of kings (Revelation 20:7-9). This worldwide revolt will prove that you cannot truly change people by changing their environment.

The change cannot be external. It must be internal, and that can happen only through the work of the Holy Spirit who is received by believers when they put their faith in Jesus as Lord and Savior (Acts 2:38 and Ephesians 1:13).

Why the Revolt?

This raises an additional question. Why would most of those living in the flesh join a revolt against God after living for a thousand years in a perfect society? Well, just stop for a moment and consider the fact that the Scriptures say Jesus will rule with a "rod of iron" (Psalm 2:9 and Revelation 2:27). This means He will dictate the law, and it will be strictly enforced by those of us in glorified bodies who will be reigning with Jesus (Revelation 2:26-27). Justice will be swift and certain.

Now, think what it would be like to live in the flesh under such a government. The fallen nature would constantly be desiring the things of the world — drugs, alcohol, promiscuous sex, gambling, etc. Yet, knowing justice is swift and certain, most people will restrain themselves and praise Jesus through clenched teeth. But once Satan is released, he will call on the frustrated, unrepentant sinners of the world to join him in overthrowing "the joker in Jerusalem."

Thus, history is going to end as it began, going in full circle. It started with two people in a perfect environment called the Garden of Eden. They rebelled against their Creator. It will end with all of humanity living in a perfect environment, the Millennium, and most of them, like Adam and Eve, will decide to revolt.

Satan's Fate

The final rebels of history will be supernaturally destroyed by God when they march on Jerusalem (Revelation 20:9). At that point, Satan will be thrown into the lake of fire (Hell) where he will be tormented day and night forever, together with his demons and the Antichrist and False Prophet (Revelation 20:10).

Notice how these revelations of God's Word dispel the mythical concept of the Middle Ages that Satan and his demons will be in charge of Hell where they will eternally torment the lost souls of Mankind. On the contrary, the Bible teaches that Hell was created for the torment of Satan and his angels (Matthew 25:41). Satan will not be the CEO of Hell. He will be a prisoner of Hell.

He will also be an object of derision. Isaiah says that the saved will be allowed to gaze upon him, and they will mock him by saying, "Is this the man who made the earth tremble, who shook kingdoms, who made the world like a wilderness and overthrew its cities?" (Isaiah 14:16-17).

Satan's Persistence and Frustration

Two final questions: Why does Satan persist in his rebellion against God? Doesn't he realize there is no hope in his attempt to dethrone the Creator of the universe?

Satan may be the great deceiver, but he himself is the most deceived being in the universe. There is no deception greater than self-deception, and Satan has convinced himself that he can ultimately triumph.

But he is doomed. No matter what he throws at God, it will be tossed right back into his face, and it will be converted to the glory of Jesus.

Consider the Cross. Satan manipulated the murder of God's Son. He thought he had achieved his greatest victory. But through the power of the Resurrection, God converted the most dastardly act of history into one of history's most glorious events.

Satan has got to be the most frustrated creature in all of God's creation. It is no wonder that Psalm 2 tells us that while Satan plots and schemes against God and His Anointed One, the Creator sits in Heaven and laughs! (Psalm 2:4). His laughter is not motivated by a lack of concern. He laughs because He has the wisdom and power to orchestrate all the evil of Satan to the triumph of His Son.

> *I am God, and there is no other;*
> *I am God, and there is no one like Me,*
> *Declaring the end from the beginning*
> *And from ancient times things which have*
> *not been done,*
> *Saying, "My purpose will be established,*
> *And I will accomplish all My good pleasure" . . .*
> *Truly I have spoken;*
> *Truly I will bring it to pass.*
> *I have planned it, surely I will do it.*
> (Isaiah 46:9b-11)

PART 4
GOOD NEWS FOR CHRISTIANS

"For the grace of God has appeared, bringing salvation to all men, instructing us to deny ungodliness and worldly desires and to live sensibly, righteously and godly in the present age, looking for the blessed hope and the appearing of the glory of our great God and Savior, Christ Jesus, who gave Himself for us to redeem us from every lawless deed, and to purify for Himself a people for His own possession, zealous for good deeds." — Titus 2:11-14

THE ESCAPE OF THE CHURCH

"Keep on the alert at all times, praying in order that you may have strength to escape all these things that are about to take place, and to stand before the Son of Man"
— Luke 21:36

There is incredibly good news for those of us who are Christians regarding the horrors of the Tribulation and the terror of the Antichrist. And that news is that God has promised that we will not have to face either one. Scriptures prophesy that all true believers will be taken out of this world before the Tribulation begins and the Antichrist is revealed.

This escape of Christians is called the Rapture. We will look first at the concept of the Rapture, and then, in the next chapter, we will consider what the Bible says about its timing.

My Personal Experience

I was born into a Christian family, and I spent my childhood going to church every time there was a function of any type — Sunday morning and evening worship, Wednesday prayer meeting, special Gospel meetings, and Vacation Bible School. I heard literally hundreds of sermons, but almost none about Bible prophecy. Never once did I ever hear the word, Rapture, mentioned.

If you had asked me at age 20 what the Rapture was, I probably would have said it's a sensation you feel when your kiss your girlfriend!

With regard to the return of the Lord, I was taught that it would occur suddenly one day without warning and that it would mark the end of the world. Those of us who were saved, both the living and dead, would go to Heaven to live with God forever.

Another word I never heard was tribulation. There was simply no teaching whatsoever that a time of great tribulation was coming upon the world and that it would produce unparalleled suffering and death.

Later in life, after I started studying Bible prophecy, I discovered that I had grown up in an Amillennial church, although I never once ever heard that word either.

As I investigated the meaning of Amillennialism, I further discovered that our Amillennial church believed that we were living in the Millennium because the Holy Spirit is in the world suppressing evil. We also believed we were simultaneously living in the Tribulation because most of the world had rejected Christ and was caught up in sin and rebellion against God.

But we never really discussed these things. We were content to focus on the present. The future was something we could not know, and there was no reason to worry about it.

We were basically prophetically ignorant, and it was easy to remain that way because I grew up in the 1940s and 50s before the existence of Christian bookstores and Christian radio and television. We lived in our own little cloistered world with little contact with those outside our denomination.

I was probably 30 years old before I encountered a brochure about the Rapture. As I read it, I began to wonder what strange cult had produced it! I was astonished when I discovered the author was a Southern Baptist. I mentioned the concept to my minister, and he scoffed, "The word Rapture is not even in the Bible."

So, I tried to dismiss the fascinating concept from my mind, but I kept running across it. Finally, I decided I would study the weird idea so that I could biblically refute it. To say the least, I was in for a surprise.

Digging into Scripture

As I started studying what the Bible had to say about the return of Jesus, I began to focus in on the only two detailed descriptions of the Lord's return that are contained in the New Testament, one written by the Apostle Paul and the other by the Apostle John. These descriptions are reproduced on the next page side by side. Stop for a moment and read them carefully.

Now, look again and make a careful comparison. Notice that they have absolutely nothing in common, except that they both focus on Jesus. Beyond that one fact, they are totally incompatible.

1 Thessalonians 4:13-18

In First Thessalonians Jesus appears in the heavens, bringing with Him the spirits of those who have died in Him. There is the blowing of a trumpet and the shout of an archangel. The dead in Christ are resurrected. Their supernaturally reconstructed bodies ascend to meet the Lord in the sky, where their spirits will be reunited with their bodies and their bodies will be glorified (see 1 Corinthians 15:42-44, 51-58). The living in Christ will follow, and on the way up, they will be translated from mortal to immortal.

In Matthew 25:6 Jesus indicates that the archangel will shout, "Behold, the Bridegroom!" That would be appropriate, for the image in First Thessalonians is that of a bridegroom coming for his bride.

The New Testament Descriptions of the Lord's Return

1 Thessalonians 4:13-18	Revelation 19:11-16
13) But we do not want you to be uninformed, brethren, about those who are asleep, that you may not grieve, as do the rest who have no hope.	11) And I saw heaven opened; and behold, a white horse, and He who sat upon it is called Faithful and True; and in righteousness He judges and wages war.
14) For if we believe that Jesus died and rose again, even so God will bring with Him those who have fallen asleep in Jesus.	12) And His eyes are a flame of fire, and upon His head are many diadems; and He has a name written upon Him which no one knows except Himself.
15) For this we say to you by the word of the Lord, that we who are alive, and remain until the coming of the Lord, shall not precede those who have fallen asleep.	13) And He is clothed with a robe dipped in blood; and His name is called The Word of God.
16) For the Lord Himself will descend from heaven with a shout, with the voice of the archangel, and with the trumpet of God; and the dead in Christ shall rise first.	14) And the armies which are in heaven, clothed in fine linen, white and clean, were following Him on white horses.
17) Then we who are alive and remain shall be caught up together with them in the clouds to meet the Lord in the air, and thus we shall always be with the Lord.	15) And from His mouth comes a sharp sword, so that with it He may smite the nations; and He will rule them with a rod of iron; and He treads the wine press of the fierce wrath of God, the Almighty.
18) Therefore comfort one another with these words.	16) And on His robe and on His thigh, He has a name written, "KING OF KINGS, AND LORD OF LORDS."

What an exciting passage! It is no wonder that it ends with the statement, "Comfort one another with these words." The dead in Christ will be resurrected and glorified (made immortal). The living in Christ will be instantly translated (changed from mortal to immortal). That means there is a whole generation of Christians who will never die — the generation that is alive at the time the Lord appears in the heavens.

Revelation 19:11-16

The image of the Lord's return contained in Revelation 19 presents a startling contrast to the one in First Thessalonians.

As Revelation 19 opens, we have come to the end of the seven years of the Great Tribulation. All the angels and saints in Heaven are shouting "Hallelujah!" because the kingdom of the Antichrist has been destroyed and the time has come for Jesus to return to the earth (Revelation 19:1-6).

But first, Jesus celebrates His union with His bride, the Church (Revelation 19:7-10). He does this by treating His bride to a great wedding feast.

At the end of this meal, the heavens open, and Jesus and His bride return to earth in glory, riding white horses (Revelation 19:11-14). He returns as a warrior to "judge and wage war" against the enemies of God. He returns as an avenger to pour out the wrath of God on those who have rejected God's love and grace. And He returns as a king to "strike down the nations" and "rule them with a rod of iron" (Revelation 19:15-16).

Comparison and Contrast

The passage in First Thessalonians presents a scene of love, mercy, and grace. The picture that is painted in Revelation is one of vengeance and wrath. In the Thessalonian passage, the Lord appears in the sky, but does not descend to the earth. In the Revelation account, He comes to the earth, in accordance with Zechariah 14 which says He will return to the Mount of Olives from which He ascended into Heaven.

One of the most significant differences between the two passages relates to the Church. In the Thessalonian account, the Lord appears for the purpose of taking His Church, both the dead and living members, out of this world. In Revelation, by stark contrast, He returns with His Church. This is indicated in Revelation 19:14 where it says that "the armies which are in heaven, clothed in fine linen, white and clean were following Him on white horses." We know these people constitute the Church, because the same group is described a few verses earlier (verses 7 and 8) as being the "bride" of Christ.

In Paul's description of the Lord's return, Jesus is portrayed as coming *for* His Church, to deliver believers from the "wrath that is to come" (1 Thessalonians 1:10). But in John's description, Jesus is portrayed as returning *with* His Church in great wrath. In Thessalonians Jesus appears as a Deliverer. In Revelation He comes back as a Warrior. In one scene He is coming to claim the righteous; in the other, He returns to condemn the unrighteous.

A Summary Comparison

1 Thessalonians 4:13-18	Revelation 19:11-16
1) Jesus appears in the heavens.	1) Jesus returns to earth.
2) Jesus comes for His Church.	2) Jesus returns with His Church.
3) Jesus is a Deliverer.	3) Jesus is a Warrior.
4) Jesus appears in grace.	4) Jesus returns in wrath.
5) Jesus appears as a bridegroom.	5) Jesus returns as a king.

A Problem of Reconciliation

What is going on here? How could these two passages be talking about the same event? How can they be reconciled?

I believe there is only one way to reconcile them and that is to conclude that ***they are describing two separate events.*** That, in turn, implies rather clearly that there are going to be *two* future comings of the Lord.

One of those — the one described in 1 Thessalonians 4 — will be more of an appearing than a coming, for the Lord will not actually return to the earth. He will, instead, appear in the heavens and supernaturally draw the Church, living and dead, to Him.

The second future appearance of the Lord — the one described in Revelation 19 — will be the true "Second Coming," for the Lord will actually descend to the earth to pour out the wrath of God and establish His reign over all the world.

This means the "Second Coming" of the Lord is going to be in two stages. The first stage will be what has come to be known as the Rapture — the snatching of the Church out of the world. The second stage, which will occur later, will be the return of the Lord to the earth.

The Issue of Imminence

This method of reconciling these passages solves a serious problem that emerges when you think of only one future coming of the Lord. That problem relates to the emphasis that the Scriptures give to *imminence.*

What I am referring to, of course, is the constant warning of the Scriptures that the Lord may appear any moment and, therefore, we are to always be ready for the Lord's return (Matthew 24:36,42,44,50 and 25:13).

If there is only one future coming of the Lord, then these warnings are a waste of time and there is no imminence because there are many prophecies that are yet to be fulfilled before the Lord can return. For example:

1) A peace treaty must be signed that will guarantee Israel's peace with all of its Arab neighbors (Daniel 9:27).

2) The Jewish temple must be rebuilt in Jerusalem (Matthew 24:15, 2 Thessalonians 2:3-4, and Revelation 11:1-2).

3) The Great Tribulation must begin and run its seven year course, resulting in the death of over half the world's population (Revelation 6-18).

4) The Antichrist must reveal himself and begin an unprecedented persecution of the Jews — one that will result in the death of two-thirds of all the Jews (Revelation 12:13-17 and Zechariah 13:7-9).

5) The Gospel must be preached to every person on the earth (Matthew 24:14 and Revelation 14:6-7).

6) An unprecedented system of economic control must be established that will prevent persons from buying or selling anything unless they can display on their right hand or forehead the number or name of the Antichrist (Revelation 13:16-18).

7) The worldwide kingdom of the Antichrist must be destroyed in "one hour of one day" (Revelation 17 and 18).

These are all events that are clearly prophesied in Scripture as occurring before Jesus returns to earth. None of them have yet been fulfilled in history. If there is only one future coming of the Lord, and it must take place after these events, then why should we be looking for Jesus Christ? We should be looking instead for the Antichrist!

Living with Expectancy

The only way that the imminence taught by the Scriptures can be maintained is to believe that Jesus can return any moment. The only way to maintain that belief is to conclude that the Lord's appearing for His Church (the Rapture) is an event that is separate and apart from the Second Coming and is an event that can occur any moment.

That is what I have concluded from my study of prophecy, and I therefore live looking for the Rapture to occur any moment. This is exactly what Paul commands us to do when he writes that we are to live "looking for the blessed hope and the appearing of the glory of our great God and Savior, Christ Jesus" (Titus 2:13).

I therefore do not believe there is one prophecy in the Bible that must be fulfilled before the Lord appears for His Church. He can appear any moment. And the imminence of His appearing becomes increasingly apparent as the signs of the time point to the events that will culminate with His Second Coming. Those signs include, among others, the reestablishment of the state of Israel, the Jewish reoccupation of the city of Jerusalem, the reunification of Europe, and the rise of Arab militancy in the Middle East.

Keep in mind that the Rapture is not the event that will kick-off the Tribulation. That event is the signing of a peace treaty that will guarantee the peace of Israel with all its Arab neighbors and will also authorize the Jews to rebuild their temple (Daniel 9:27). The Rapture could occur years before the Tribulation begins, although it is most likely to occur near the beginning because the Tribulation is the time for the pouring out of God's wrath, and 1 Thessalonians 1:10 says that Jesus will "deliver" His Church "from the wrath to come."

A Signless Event

Since the Rapture is imminent, and always has been, there are no signs that point to it. The signs of the times that the Bible gives us to watch for relate to the Tribulation and the Second Coming. But when those signs start accumulating, as they are doing so today, we can be assured that the Rapture is going to occur any moment.

I once heard Tim LaHaye describe the relationship between the Rapture and the signs of the times in a very unique way. He said he and his wife were walking through a shopping mall when she suddenly stopped him and said, "Look around and tell me what you see."

Tim surveyed the mall, and responded, "The only thing I see that is different from normal is people putting up Christmas decorations."

"That's right," she said, "and what is that a sign of?"

"Well," Tim responded, "it's a sign that Christmas is coming soon."

"Yes," she replied, "but it is also a sign that Thanksgiving is right around the corner!"

In like manner, we see increasing signs today which indicate the Tribulation is about to begin. And that means the Rapture is "right around the corner."

A Biblical Concept

I hope I have been able to prove to you conclusively that the concept of the Rapture is a biblical one. In that regard, I think I should point out that it is mentioned in more places than just 1 Thessalonians 4.

The first clear mention of the Rapture in Scripture is found in the words of Jesus recorded in John 14:1-4. Jesus said, "I will come again, and receive you to Myself; that where I am, there you may be also."

As we have seen, the Apostle Paul gives us the most detailed description of the Rapture in 1 Thessalonians 4:13-18. But that is not his only reference to the event. Paul mentions the Rapture again in 1 Corinthians 15 — his famous chapter on the resurrection of the dead:

> Behold, I tell you a mystery; we shall not all sleep, but we shall be changed, in a moment, in the twinkling of an eye, at the last trumpet. (verses 51 and 52)

Paul's reference here to being changed is an allusion to the fact that at the time of the Rapture the saints will receive glorified bodies that will be imperishable, immortal, and perfected (1 Corinthians 15:42-44, 50-55 and Isaiah 35:5-6).

Another reference Paul makes to the Rapture can be found in 1 Thessalonians 1:10 where he wrote that we are "to wait for His Son from heaven, whom He raised from the dead, that is Jesus, who delivers us from the wrath to come." And in his letter to the church at Philippi, Paul said, "I press on toward the goal for the prize of the upward call of God in Christ Jesus" (Philippians 3:14).

Jesus mentioned the Rapture again when He appeared to John on the Isle of Patmos some 65 years after His death, burial and resurrection. In chapters 2 and 3 of Revelation we have seven letters to seven different churches which Jesus dictated to John. In one of those letters, the one addressed to the church in Philadelphia, Jesus said, "Because you have kept the word of My perseverance, I also will keep you from the hour of testing, that hour which is about to come upon the whole world, to test those who dwell upon the earth" (Revelation 3:10).

Old Testament Silence

Some often ask why the Rapture is not mentioned in the Hebrew Scriptures. After all, there are many references to the Second Coming in the Old Testament.

The answer to this question is very easy. The concept of the Rapture was not revealed to the Old Testament prophets because it is a promise to the New Testament Church and not to the saints of God who lived before the establishment of the Church. Jesus will return as a bridegroom for His bride, and that bride consists only of Church Age saints.

The saints of Old Testament times will be resurrected at the end of the Tribulation and not at the time of the Rapture of the Church. Daniel reveals this fact in Daniel 12:1-2 where he says that the saints of that age will be resurrected at the end of the "time of distress."

The Biblical Validity of the Term

I told you earlier that my initial interest in the Rapture was cut short when my pastor told me that the term was not even in the Bible. This is an argument I have heard many times since.

The first thing we need to keep in mind is that there are many biblical concepts that are not mentioned by name in the Bible. The Trinity is a good example. It is a concept that is clearly taught, but the word is never mentioned. The word was coined by theologians to express a biblical truth. The same is true of the Shekinah. That term was coined by Hebrew theologians to express the concept of the manifest glory of God on earth, something that is referred to many times in the Bible.

Likewise, the word, Rapture, expresses a biblical concept. But what most people do not realize is that the word is actually in the Scriptures. It can be found in the Latin Vulgate translation of the Bible in 1 Thessalonians 4:17 where Paul writes that when Jesus appears in the heavens, the living in Christ will be "caught up" to meet Him in the clouds. The term, caught up, is expressed in the Latin version with the word *rapio* which means to catch up, to snatch away, or to take out.

A word does not have to appear in an English translation of the Bible for it to be a biblical word. The Latin Vulgate translation of Jerome served as the Bible of Western Civilization for over 1,000 years, from the 5th Century to the 16th. In contrast, the King James Version has been around only 400 years.

Escapism

One criticism I constantly hear about the Rapture is that it is nothing in the world but an unfounded hope on the part of those who are not willing to suffer for the Lord. Believers in the Rapture are thus often labeled as "Escapists."

We should understand that the Bible makes it clear that anyone who truly stands for Jesus Christ in this wicked world is going to suffer persecution and tribulation (2 Timothy 3:12). But the Great Tribulation is another matter. Its purpose is to pour out the wrath of God on those who have rejected His Son, Jesus, and that, of course, does not include the Church.

Furthermore, Jesus specifically promised believers that they would be rescued from the Great Tribulation. His words are recorded in Luke 21:36 —

> . . . keep on the alert at all times, praying that you may have strength to ***escape*** all these things that are about to take place, and to

stand before the Son of Man. (Emphasis added.)

The Newness of the Concept

Let me address one last objection to the Rapture. It is one I hear all the time: "It's too new to be true."

There are several problems with this argument. The first is that it ignores the fact that the Bible teaches that end time prophecies will not be understood until the time comes for the predicted events to take place.

When the prophet Daniel was given some specific prophecies about the end times, he complained to the Lord that he did not understand them. The Lord responded with these words: "Go your way, Daniel, for these words are concealed and sealed up until the end times" (Daniel 12:9). Jeremiah was told the same thing by the Lord on two occasions (Jeremiah 23:20 and 30:24).

There are many end time prophecies that cannot be understood apart from historical or technological developments. For example, all of end time prophecy revolves around the state of Israel. Those prophecies were not fully understandable before the re-establishment of the state of Israel in May of 1948. Think of it for a moment — how could anyone in 1900 understand the prophecy in Ezekiel 38 that Russia will invade Israel in the end times? Israel did not exist, nor was there any prospect of Israel ever existing again. And Russia was a peaceful Christian Orthodox country.

In like manner, before modern times, how could anyone understand the prophecy in Revelation 11 about the killing and resurrection of the two witnesses of God? That prophecy says that the whole world will look upon their bodies and witness their resurrection and rapture to Heaven (Revelation 11:9-12). No one could understand this prophecy before the development of satellite television communication in the

1960s.

In summary, the Bible clearly teaches that the understanding of end time prophecy will be progressive in nature. We will understand more of the prophecies the closer we get to the time of their fulfillment.

A Delayed Discovery

In this regard, the reason the concept of the Rapture was delayed in its development until the 19th Century was because the Roman Catholic Church adopted St. Augustine's Amillennial viewpoint of prophecy hook-line-and-sinker around 430 AD. In his book, *The City of God*, Augustine spiritualized Bible prophecy and then argued that the Millennium began at the Cross and would continue until the Second Coming. He had no concept of the Rapture.

This spiritualizing approach to the interpretation of Bible prophecy proceeded to dominate theology for the next thousand years. During that period of time any disagreement with Church doctrine was considered heresy and was punishable by death. And those branded as heretics usually had all their writings destroyed by the Church.

So, there is no way of knowing how many people during that time may have discerned the difference in the Scriptures between the Rapture and the Second Coming. Of course, another thing that kept people from serious study of the Bible was the fact that most of the general public was illiterate and few had any access to a Bible.

Protestants adopted the spiritualizing approach to prophecy after the Reformation and expressed it in the Postmillennial view that emerged in the mid-17th Century. Both Amillennialism and Postmillennialism are based on the assumption that Bible prophecy does not mean what it says.

The Revival of Literal Interpretation

The discovery of the distinction which the Bible makes between the Rapture and the Second Coming had to await the revival of the application of literal interpretation to Bible prophecy. I say "revival" because the writings of the Church Fathers during the first 300 years of church history (100 AD to 400 AD) reveal that they interpreted prophecy for its plain sense meaning. Accordingly, they were nearly all Premillennialists. In fact, Justin Martyr (110-165 AD) went so far as to suggest that anyone with a different viewpoint was heretical.[1]

The revival of literal interpretation began in earnest among the Puritans in the 17th Century, and it quickly led to an understanding that the Rapture would be an event separate from and preceding the Second Coming. Puritan leader, Increase Mather (1639-1723), argued "that the saints would be caught up into the air" and thus escape the world's final conflagration.[2]

Most people I encounter seem to believe that the concept of the Rapture originated in the writings of C. I. Scofield, as expressed in his famous study Bible that was published in 1909.[3] It is true that Scofield's writing helped to popularize the idea, but he was by no means the originator of it.

Paul N. Benware, in his book, *Understanding End Times Prophecy*, notes that many writers in the 17th and 18th Centuries began to speak of a Rapture separate and apart from the Second Coming:[4]

> Peter Jurieu in his book, *Approaching Deliverance of the Church* (1687) taught that Christ would come in the air to rapture the saints and return to Heaven before the battle of Armageddon . . . Philip Doddridge's commentary on the New Testament (1738) and John Gill's commentary on the New Testament (1748)

> both use the term rapture and speak of it as imminent. It is clear these men believed that this coming will precede Christ's descent to the earth and the time of judgment. The purpose was to preserve believers from the time of judgment. James Macknight (1763) and Thomas Scott (1792) taught that the righteous will be carried to heaven, where they will be secure until the time of judgment is over.

A Final Question

This leaves us with a final question: "When is the Rapture most likely to happen?" This question has been hotly debated, even among those who believe in the Rapture.

Specifically, the question relates to whether or not the Rapture will occur before the Tribulation, in the middle of the Tribulation, or near the end of that terrible period in human history. This is a question that I will address in detail in the next chapter.

A Summary

Let's conclude with a summary. The Rapture passages in the New Testament teach this glorious event will begin with the shout of an archangel and the blowing of a trumpet. Jesus will suddenly appear in the heavens, bringing with Him the spirits of Church Age believers who have already died. The bodies of the dead in Christ will be resurrected and rise up to meet the Lord in the sky. He will put their spirits back into their bodies and glorify them, making them immortal. Then, those saints who are alive will be "caught up" to the Lord. On the way up, they will be transformed from mortal to immortal. Jesus will then return to Heaven with all His Church Age saints in their glorified bodies.

Paul concludes his description of the Rapture in 1 Thessalonians 4 by encouraging his readers to "comfort one another with these words." What a comfort they are, but what a tragedy it is that most professing Christians, both Catholic and Protestant, know nothing about the Rapture and therefore cannot rest in the comfort of its promise.

All my life I have heard that there are two things no one can avoid: taxes and death. Well, that is not true. According to 1 Thessalonians 4, a whole generation of believers — those alive at the time of the Rapture — will escape death. Taxes appear to be the only inevitability!

Hope or Terror?

We should be looking for two future comings of the Lord. The first, the Rapture, will be the appearing of the Lord for His Church. The second, the Second Coming, will be the return of the Lord to the earth to "judge and wage war" against the enemies of God (Revelation 19:11), and to establish His thousand year reign (Revelation 20).

The signs of the times point to the fact that we are on the threshold of the Tribulation. The Jews are back in their land and their sacred city, and the whole world is coming against them over the issue of the control of Jerusalem. Jesus must be at the very gates of Heaven, waiting for His Father's command to appear for His Church. The Rapture is imminent.

Let's consider now when it is most likely to occur.

THE TIMING OF THE ESCAPE

". . . wait for His Son from heaven, whom He raised from the dead, that is Jesus, who delivers us from the wrath to come."
— 1 Thessalonians 1:10

When is the Rapture most likely to occur? This is a very controversial issue because the timing of the Rapture is not specifically stated in the Scriptures. We are simply told repeatedly that it is imminent, meaning it could happen at any moment.

Specific concepts of timing — whether it will happen before, during, or at the end of the Tribulation — must be based upon inferences of Scripture, and thus there is room for honest differences of opinion. Lines of fellowship should never be drawn over differences regarding this point, even though it is an important point.

Let's begin our search for the timing of the Rapture by taking a look at all the various viewpoints.

The Post-Tribulation Rapture

Those who place the timing of the Rapture at the end of the Tribulation attempt to combine the Rapture with the Second Coming. In their view, the Lord will appear in the heavens for His Church, and then, after the living and dead in Christ have been gathered, the Lord will either immediately return to heaven with them (the Amillennial view) or return with them to earth (a variant of the Premillennial view). The latter concept is often derisively referred to as the "Yo-yo

Rapture," since it pictures the saints rising to meet the Lord in the air and then immediately returning to earth with Him.

Those who place the timing of the Rapture at the end of the Tribulation usually base their argument on two parables in Matthew 13 and on the Lord's Olivet Discourse in Matthew 24.

In Matthew 24 the Lord portrays His gathering of the saints as an event that will take place "immediately after the tribulation of those days" (Matthew 24:29). This certainly sounds like a post-Tribulation Rapture. But it must be kept in mind that the book of Matthew was written to the Jews, and therefore the recording of Jesus' speech by Matthew has a distinctively Jewish flavor to it as compared to Luke's record of the same speech.

Note, for example, Matthew's references to Judea and to Jewish law regarding travel on the Sabbath (Matthew 24:15-20). These are omitted in Luke's account. Instead, Luke speaks of the saints looking up for deliverance "to escape all these things" when the end time signs "begin to take place" (Luke 21:28, 36). The saints in Matthew are instructed to flee from Judea and hide. The saints in Luke are told to look up for deliverance.

It appears, therefore, that Matthew and Luke are speaking of two different sets of saints. The saints in Matthew's account are most likely Jews (and Gentiles)who receive Jesus as their Messiah during the Tribulation. The saints in Luke are those who receive Christ before the Tribulation begins. Most of those who accept the Lord during the Tribulation will be martyred (Revelation 7:9-14). Those who live to the end will be gathered by the angels of the Lord (Matthew 24:31).

The parable of the wheat and tares (Matthew 13:24-30) and the parable of the dragnet (Matthew 13:47-50) can be explained in the same way. They refer to a separation of saints and sinners that will take place at the end of the Tribulation. The saints are those who receive Jesus as their Savior during the Tribulation (Gentile and Jew) and who live to the end of that awful period.

As I demonstrated in the previous chapter, the Bible clearly teaches that the Rapture is an event that is separate and apart from the Second Coming. The two simply cannot be combined into one event.

The Mid-Tribulation Rapture

There are variations of the mid-Tribulation Rapture concept. The most common is that the Church will be taken out in the exact middle of the Tribulation, at the point in time when the Antichrist reveals himself in Jerusalem..

This concept is based upon a statement in 1 Corinthians 15:52 which says that the Rapture will occur at the blowing of "the last trumpet." This trumpet is then identified with the seventh trumpet of the trumpet judgments in the book of Revelation. Since the blowing of the seventh trumpet is recorded in Revelation 11, the mid-point of the Tribulation, the conclusion is that the Rapture must occur in the middle of the Tribulation.

But there are two problems with this interpretation. The first is that the last trumpet of 1 Corinthians 15 is blown for believers whereas the seven trumpets of Revelation 8, 9 and 11 are sounded for unbelievers. The Revelation trumpets have no relevance for the Church. The last trumpet of 1 Corinthians 15 is a trumpet for the righteous. The last trumpet for the unrighteous is the one described in Revelation 11.

Another problem with this interpretation is that the passage in Revelation 11 that portrays the sounding of the seventh trumpet is a "flash forward" to the end of the Tribulation. Flash forwards are very common in the book of Revelation. They occur after something terrible is described in order to assure the reader that everything is going to turn out all right when Jesus returns at the end of the Tribulation.

Thus, the eighth and ninth chapters of Revelation, which describe the horrors of the trumpet judgments, are followed immediately by a flash forward in chapter 10 that pictures the return of Jesus in victory at the end of the Tribulation. The mid-Tribulation action resumes in chapter 11 with a description of the killing of the two great prophets of God by the Antichrist. Then, to offset that terrible event, we are presented with another flash forward, beginning with verse 15. The seventh trumpet is sounded and we find ourselves propelled forward to the end of the Tribulation when "the kingdom of the world becomes the kingdom of our Lord."

The point is that the seventh trumpet of Revelation relates to the end of the Tribulation and not the middle. It is the same trumpet that is referred to in Matthew 24:31, the trumpet that will be blown to announce the Second Coming of Jesus. It is therefore no basis for an argument in behalf of a mid-Tribulation Rapture.

The Pre-Wrath Rapture

A variation of the mid-Tribulation Rapture is the pre-wrath Rapture concept that places the Rapture at the beginning of the last quarter of the Tribulation, about five and a half years into the Tribulation.

The argument for this view is that the Church is promised protection only from the wrath of God and not the wrath of Man or of Satan. It is then argued that only the bowl judgments in the last quarter of the Tribulation (Revelation 16) represent the wrath of God.

But the argument for this view disintegrates when you consider two facts. First, it is Jesus Himself who breaks the seals that launch each of the seal judgments recorded in Revelation 6. These judgments occur at the beginning of the

Tribulation. Second, the seven angels who blow the trumpets that initiate each of the trumpet judgments are given their trumpets at the throne of God (Revelation 8:2).

All the judgments of Revelation are clearly superintended by God. That is the reason we are told in Revelation 15:1 that the bowl judgments at the end of the Tribulation will finish the wrath of God, not begin His wrath.

The Pre-Tribulation Rapture

I believe the best inference of Scripture is that the Rapture will occur before the beginning of the Tribulation. The most important reason I believe this has to do with the issue of imminence.

Over and over in Scripture we are told to watch for the appearing of the Lord. We are told "to be ready" (Matthew 24:44), "to be on the alert" (Matthew 24:42), "to be dressed in readiness" (Luke 12:35), and to "keep your lamps alight" (Luke 12:35). The clear force of these persistent warnings is that Jesus can appear at any moment.

Only the pre-Tribulation concept of the Rapture allows for the imminence of the Lord's appearing for His Church. When the Rapture is placed at any other point in time, the imminence of the Lord's appearing is destroyed because other prophetic events must happen first.

For example, if the Rapture is going to occur in mid-Tribulation, then why should I live looking for the Lord's appearing at any moment? I would be looking instead for an Israeli peace treaty, the rebuilding of the Temple, and the revelation of the Antichrist. Then and only then could the Lord appear.

Our Focus

This raises the issue of what we are to be looking for. Nowhere are Christian believers told to watch for the appearance of the Antichrist. On the contrary, we are told to watch for Jesus Christ. In Titus 2:13 Paul says we are to live "looking for the blessed hope and the appearing of the glory of our great God and Savior, Christ Jesus." Likewise, Peter urges us to "fix our hope completely on the grace to be brought to us at the revelation of Jesus Christ" (1 Peter 1:13). John completes the apostolic chorus by similarly urging us to "fix our hope on Him" at His appearing (1 John 3:2-3).

In Matthew 24:15 Jesus speaks of watching for the Antichrist, but He is speaking to Jews and is warning them to flee Jerusalem when the Antichrist comes to that city in the middle of the Tribulation.

Wrath

Another argument in behalf of a pre-Tribulation Rapture has to do with the promises of God to protect the Church from His wrath. As has already been demonstrated, the book of Revelation shows that the wrath of God will be poured out during the entire period of the Tribulation.

The Word promises over and over that the Church will be delivered from God's wrath. Romans 5:9 says that "we shall be saved from the wrath of God through Him [Jesus]." First Thessalonians 1:10 states that we are waiting "for His Son from heaven . . . who will deliver us from the wrath to come." The promise is repeated in 1 Thessalonians 5:9 — "God has not destined us for wrath, but for obtaining salvation through our Lord Jesus Christ."

Deliverance

Some argue that God could supernaturally protect the Church during the Tribulation. Yes, He could. In fact, He promises to do just that for the 144,000 Jews who will be sealed as bond-servants at the beginning of the Tribulation (Revelation 7:1-8).

But God's promise to the Church during the Tribulation is not one of protection but one of deliverance. Jesus said we would "escape" the horrors of the Tribulation (Luke 21:36). Paul says Jesus is coming to "deliver" us from God's wrath (1 Thessalonians 1:10).

Paul's Assurance

An interesting argument in behalf of the pre-Tribulation timing of the Rapture can be found in 2 Thessalonians. The church at Thessalonica was in a turmoil because someone had written them a letter under Paul's name stating that they had missed the "gathering to the Lord" and were, in fact, living in "the day of the Lord" (2 Thessalonians 2:1-2).

Paul attempted to calm them down by reminding them of his teaching that "the day of the Lord" (the Tribulation) would not come until after the Antichrist is revealed. He then stated that the Antichrist would not be revealed until a restraining force "is taken out of the way" (2 Thessalonians 2:3-7).

There has been much speculation as to the identity of this restraining force that Paul refers to. Some have identified it as the Holy Spirit. But it cannot be the Holy Spirit because there will be people saved during the Tribulation, and no one can be saved apart from the testimony of the Spirit (John 16:8-11 and 1 John 5:7).

Others have identified the restrainer as human government. It is true that government was ordained by God to restrain evil (Romans 13:1-4). But the governments of the world are in rebellion against God and His Son (Psalm 2), and they are therefore a contributor to the evil that characterizes the world. Furthermore, the Tribulation will not be characterized by a lack of government. Rather, it will feature the first true worldwide government (Revelation 13:7).

In my opinion that leaves only one other candidate for Paul's restrainer — and that is the Church. It is the Church that serves as the primary restrainer of evil in the world today as it proclaims the Gospel and stands for righteousness. When the Church fails in this mission, evil multiplies, as Paul graphically points out in 2 Timothy 3:1-5. Paul says that society in the end times will be characterized by chaos and despair because "men will hold to a form of religion but will deny its power." When the Church is removed from the world, all hell will literally break loose.

Symbolic Evidence in the Old Testament

There are several prophetic types that seem to affirm the concept of deliverance from Tribulation.

Take Enoch for example. He was a prophet to the Gentiles who was raptured out of the world before God poured out His wrath in the great flood of Noah's time. Enoch appears to be a type of the Gentile Church that will be taken out of the world before God pours out His wrath again. If so, then Noah and his family are a type of the Jewish remnant that will be protected through the Tribulation.

Another Old Testament symbolic type which points toward a pre-Tribulation Rapture is the experience of Lot and his family. They were delivered out of Sodom and Gomorrah before those cities were destroyed.

The apostle Peter alludes to both of these examples in his second epistle. He states that if God spared Noah and Lot, then He surely "knows how to rescue the godly from trial and to keep the unrighteous under punishment for the day of judgment" (2 Peter 2:9).

Another beautiful prophetic type is to be found in the Jewish wedding traditions of Jesus' time. After the betrothal, the groom would return to his father's house to prepare a wedding chamber for his bride. He would return for his bride at an unexpected moment, so the bride had to be ready constantly. When he returned, he would take his bride back to his father's house to the chamber he had prepared. He and his bride would then be sealed in the chamber for seven days. When they emerged, a great wedding feast would be celebrated.

Likewise, Jesus has returned to Heaven to prepare a place for His bride, the Church (John 14:1-4). When He returns for His bride, He will take her to His Father's heavenly home. There He will remain with His bride for seven years (the duration of the Tribulation). The period will end with "the marriage supper of the Lamb" described in Revelation 19. Thus the seven days in the wedding chamber point prophetically to the seven years that Jesus and His bride will remain in Heaven during the Tribulation.

Symbolic Evidence in the New Testament

The structure of the book of Revelation also implies a pre-Tribulation Rapture in a symbolic sense.

The first three chapters focus on the Church. Chapter 4 begins with the door of Heaven opening and John being raptured from the Isle of Patmos to the throne of God in Heaven. The Church is not mentioned thereafter until Revelation 19:7-9 when it is portrayed as the "bride of Christ" in Heaven with Jesus celebrating the "marriage supper of the Lamb." At Revelation 19:11 the door of Heaven opens again, and Jesus emerges riding a white horse on His way to earth, followed by His Church (Revelation 19:14).

The rapture of the Apostle John in Revelation 4 appears to be a symbolic type of the Rapture of the Church. Note that it is initiated by the cry of a voice that sounds like the blowing of a trumpet (Revelation 4:1). Since the Tribulation does not begin until Revelation 6, the rapture of John in Revelation 4 appears to be a symbolic type that points to a pre-Tribulation Rapture of the Church.

Some counter this argument by pointing out that although the Church is not mentioned in Revelation during that book's description of the Tribulation, there is constant mention of "saints" (for example, Revelation 13:7). But that term is not used in the Bible exclusively to refer to members of the Church. Daniel uses it to refer to Old Testament believers who lived long before the Church was established (Daniel 7:18). The saints referred to in the book of Revelation are those people who will be saved during the Tribulation, after the Church has been taken out of the world.

Logical Evidence

The Bible teaches that when Jesus returns, He is going to judge all people on earth and consign unbelievers to death. The judgment of the Gentiles is portrayed in Matthew 25:31-46; the judgment of the Jews, in Ezekiel 20:33-38. In Luke 17:37 we are told that the bodies of unbelievers will be fed to the vultures. Revelation 19:17 calls this "the supper of God." It is presented in contrast to the marriage feast of the Lamb to which believers will be invited (Revelation 19:6-10).

Once these judgments are completed, all believers left alive at the end of the Tribulation — both Jews and Gentiles — will be allowed to enter the Millennium in the flesh. This group will then begin to propagate, and through them, the earth will be re-populated. These are the people that the glorified saints will reign over for a thousand years. Since death will be curtailed and life spans will be extended during the Millennium, the population of the earth will grow exponentially.

Now, if the Rapture is combined with the Second Coming as all one event at the end of the Tribulation, then all believers will be glorified and there will be no one left in the flesh to enter the Millennium! The only way to come up with a

Millennial population is to place the Rapture before the Tribulation. Those saved during the Tribulation, and who live to the end of it, would then go into the Millennium in the flesh and serve as the nucleus group to repopulate the world.

The Purpose of the Tribulation

Another argument based upon logic is the fact that there is no purpose for the Church to be on the earth during the Tribulation. The purpose of the Tribulation is to provide a period of time for the pouring out of God's wrath. The Church is immune to the wrath of God (1 Thessalonians 1:10). There will be people saved during the Tribulation, but they will be saved by the witness of the Holy Spirit through reading the Bible, experiencing the Tribulation judgments, and hearing the messages of God's two special witnesses in Jerusalem. Also, God is going to send forth an angel at the end of the Tribulation who will circumnavigate the earth, proclaiming the Gospel one last time to every living being (Revelation 14:6-7).

Some have argued that the Church must go through the Tribulation in order to purify it for its presentation to the Lord. But true Christians need no such purification, for their sins have been purged by the blood of Jesus. Asserting that this is a purpose of the Tribulation has the effect of converting that time period into a Protestant Purgatory!

Furthermore, it makes no sense to say that Jesus is going to beat up His bride for seven years during the Tribulation before coming to fetch her for the wedding! What kind of bridegroom would do such a thing? What bride would look forward lovingly to being united to such a bridegroom?

Counter Arguments

The first rebuttal argument that is usually presented by people who reject the Pre-Tribulation Rapture is their contention that there is no mention of the Rapture in Matthew

24 where Jesus presents a sweeping survey of end time events. The Tribulation is described by the Lord in detail in verses 9-24. Then we are told in verses 25-31 that "immediately after the Tribulation," the Lord will return and will "send forth His angels to gather together His elect." Where is the Rapture?

Again, we must keep in mind that the book of Matthew was written to the Jews, and Matthew's recording of Jesus' speech in chapter 24 focuses on the Jews in the Tribulation, not the Church. As to the saints who will be gathered at the end of the Tribulation when Jesus returns, they will be those who are saved during the Tribulation, after the Rapture of the Church.

Keep Reading!

But Matthew 24 does not end with the description of the Lord's Second Coming. In verse 36 the writer suddenly shifts gears and starts recording the words of Jesus concerning an event that has to be something other than the Second Coming. He quotes Jesus saying, "But of that day and hour no one knows, not even the angels in heaven, nor the Son, but the Father alone."

This could not be a reference to the Second Coming because the Bible makes it crystal clear that Jesus will return to this earth exactly seven years after the Tribulation begins. It seems apparent that at this point in Jesus' discourse, He shifts His focus from the Second Coming to the Rapture.

Further evidence that this is true can be found in the next verse (verse 37). Jesus says, "For the coming of the Son of Man will be just like the days of Noah." He proceeds to explain that when the flood occurred, people were going about their daily lives with no sense of concern, "marrying and giving in marriage" (verses 38-44). This is anything but a description of the nature of society at the end of the Tribulation. By that time, the whole earth will be engulfed in chaos.

People will be in a perpetual state of panic rather than going about their lives in peace and calm.

So, the Rapture can be found in Matthew 24, in verses 36-44. And two times in this section of the chapter, Jesus warns to "be on the alert for you do not know which day your Lord is coming" (verses 42 and 44). Once again, since the day of the Second Coming can be precisely determined, this passage must be speaking of the Rapture and the fact that it is an imminent event that could occur any moment.

The Newness of the Concept

Another common rebuttal to the Pre-Tribulation Rapture is that it is "too new to be true." This argument is based on the assumption that the concept of a Rapture separate and apart from the Second Coming was not developed until the early 1800s by the Plymouth Brethren in England.

This assumption is not entirely correct. We know, as a matter of fact, that there were people throughout Church history who advocated a Rapture separate and apart from the Second Coming.

But even if it were true, it would not invalidate the concept. That's because — as I pointed out in the previous chapter — the Bible makes it clear that Bible prophecy will not be fully understood until the end times (Daniel 12:9).

Modern day historical events, like the re-establishment of Israel, and modern day technological developments, like the invention of nuclear power, are helping us to understand Bible prophecies that have never been understood before.

But the most important key has been the revival of literal interpretation. From 400 AD to about 1700, Bible prophecy was spiritualized and interpreted allegorically. Many new discoveries have been made in Bible prophecy since the 1700s, simply because people started accepting the prophecies to mean what they say. So, we are not talking about novel new truths. We are talking instead about the discovery of truths that were always in the Scriptures but which were muddled by spiritualization.

The Origin of Pre-Trib Viewpoint

One of the early Church Fathers, The Shepherd of Hermas, writing in the early 2nd Century, made an interesting observation about "the great tribulation that is coming." He wrote, "If then ye prepare yourselves, and repent with all your heart and turn to the Lord, it will be possible for you to escape it [the Tribulation], if your heart be pure and spotless, and ye spend the rest of the days of your life in serving the Lord blamelessly."[1]

In medieval times evidence of pretribulational thinking can be found in the recently discovered sermon attributed to Ephraem the Syrian.[2] This sermon, which was written sometime between the 4th and 6th Centuries, encourages believers to prepare themselves for meeting the Lord because "all the saints and elect of God are gathered, prior to the tribulation that is to come, and are taken to the Lord lest they see the confusion that is to overwhelm the world because of our sins." Scholars believe this text was derived from the writings of the original Ephraem who lived from 306 to 373 AD. He was one of the leading theologians of the early Byzantine Church.[3]

It is very likely that there were always some forms of premillennialism and pretribulational thought throughout the Middle Ages but, if so, these viewpoints had to be expressed underground because they violated Catholic dogma. Sects like the Albigenses, Lombards, and the Waldenses were attracted to a literal interpretation of the Bible, but little is known about their detailed beliefs because the Catholic Church declared their writings to be heretical and destroyed them.

Tommy Ice, the director of the Pre-Trib Research Center, asserts that the first person to spell out in detail the idea that the Rapture would occur before the Tribulation begins was a Baptist leader named Morgan Edwards.[4] This remarkable man was born in Wales and preached at churches in England and Ireland before emigrating to the United States in 1761 to become pastor of a church in Philadelphia. He proceeded to become the founder of Brown University and was recognized as the leading Baptist historian of his day.

As early as the 1740s Edwards was espousing a Rapture separate and apart from the Second Coming in his writings about eschatology. The difference in his view and the modern Pre-Trib concept is that he believed the Rapture would occur in the middle of Daniel's 70th week, about 3½ years before the Second Coming.

The Modern Concept

The person who crystallized the modern Pre-Trib viewpoint was a man named John Darby (1800-1882).[5] Darby was born in London and was trained in the law. He practiced law for only one year before he was overcome by a deep spiritual struggle that finally led to a decision to enter the ministry. He became an Anglican priest but quickly became disillusioned when the church decreed that all converts would have to swear allegiance to the King of England. Darby considered this to be a compromise with the lordship of Christ.

Darby decided to leave the Anglican Church. In the years following, he and other dissenters from the established state church inaugurated a movement that came to be known as the Plymouth Brethren.

In 1826 Darby broke one of his legs, and during the long convalescence that followed, he engaged in an intensive study of the Scriptures that convinced him of the clear distinction between the Church and Israel. He also became convicted of the imminent return of Jesus. Thus, by 1827 he had developed the fundamental principles that would come to characterize a new theological system that would be called Dispensationalism.

The Dissemination of the View

After John Darby refined the concept of the Pre-Tribulation Rapture, it spread rapidly throughout Europe and America. The viewpoint has always been blessed by gifted communicators. In 1878 the very first best-selling prophecy book incorporated the idea. It was *Jesus is Coming* by William E. Blackstone (1841-1935).[6] In 1909 *The Scofield Study Bible* developed the scriptural arguments for the viewpoint in detail.[7] Then came the amazing charts and diagrams of Clarence Larkin (1850-1924) in his book *Dispensational Truth*.[8]

Harry Ironside (1876-1951), the popular pastor of the Moody Memorial Church in Chicago, preached the concept in his sermons and books during the 1930s and 40s.[9] In 1970 Hal Lindsey published *The Late Great Planet Earth* and once again the viewpoint was expressed in a best seller.[10] The 20th Century ended with the view being espoused in the *Left Behind* block-buster series of books written by Tim LaHaye and Jerry Jenkins.[11]

Attacks on the View

Over the years there have been many attacks on the Pre-Trib viewpoint. The most sustained — and the most ridiculous — has been the one launched in the 1970s by Dave MacPherson.[12] In a book he keeps re-publishing under different sensational titles, MacPherson argues that the whole notion of a Pre-Tribulation Rapture was supposedly given to Darby when he attended a Charismatic prayer meeting in Scotland in 1830 where a 15 year old girl, Margaret MacDonald, went into a state of ecstasy during which she declared there would be a Rapture prior to the Tribulation. MacPherson asserts: "Darby borrowed from her, modified her views, and then popularized them under his own name without giving her credit."[13]

The first problem with MacPherson's assertions is that we know that Darby developed his concept of the Rapture's timing in the winter of 1826-1827, some three years before the prayer meeting in Scotland. The second problem relates to a strange aspect of MacPherson's book. In an appendix, he reproduces Margaret MacDonald's handwritten account of what she said at the 1830 meeting, and there is nothing in it that even suggests a Pre-Tribulation Rapture![14]

But the biggest problem with MacPherson's assertion is that it is really irrelevant. The crucial question is not where the Pre-Tribulation Rapture concept originated; rather, the only question that matters is whether or not it is biblical.

Concluding Observations

Two final observations before I conclude. First, there is a mistaken idea that only Dispensationalists believe in a Pre-Trib Rapture. That is not so. In the 1920s the view was adopted by many Pentecostal denominations such as the Assemblies of God. Today, the view is held by people in a great variety of denominations, even though their denominational leaders might not endorse it. I personally am a good example of a person who holds to the Pre-Trib viewpoint but who is not a full-blown Dispensationalist.

My final observation is that I am not dogmatic about the timing of the Rapture. Unlike some of my colleagues who are downright uncompromising about the timing, I prefer to say that "I believe the best inference of Scripture is that the Rapture is most likely to occur before the Tribulation begins." The Bible never precisely states when the Rapture will occur, and there is, therefore, legitimate room for differences of opinion.

But as for me, I believe with all my heart that the Rapture will occur before the Tribulation begins, based not on emotion or wishful thinking, but on the Scriptures. And because I believe it so strongly, I greet each new day with the words, "Maranatha! Come quickly, Lord Jesus!" (1 Corinthians 16: 22).

PART 5
ARE YOU READY?

"'For behold, the day is coming, burning like a furnace; and all the arrogant and every evildoer will be chaff; and the day that is coming will set them ablaze,' says the LORD of hosts, 'so that it will leave them neither root nor branch. But for you who fear My name, the sun of righteousness will rise with healing in its wings; and you will go forth and skip about like calves from the stall. You will tread down the wicked, for they will be ashes under the soles of your feet on the day which I am preparing,' says the LORD of hosts." — Malachi 4:1-3

EPILOGUE

"He who believes in the Son has eternal life; but he who does not obey the Son shall not see life, but the wrath of God abides on him."
— John 3:36

Are you ready for the Lord's return? If He were to appear in the heavens today for His Church, would you be taken out of this world, or would you be left behind to face the horrors of the Tribulation and the terror of the Antichrist?

Maybe you are thinking, "I probably would go because I was born into a Christian family." Or maybe your feeling is, "I'm almost positive I would go because I was baptized as a kid, and I've attended church at least once a year since then." Or perhaps you are one of the majority of people who respond to this question by saying, "Well, I've never been very religious, and I don't go to church, but I'm not a bad person, and I am certainly a lot better than most of the people I know — I mean, I'm not caught up in any serious sins."

If any of these thoughts are yours, then you need to face up to some grim realities:

- You cannot be saved by being born into a Christian family.
- You cannot be saved by performing certain religious rituals.
- You cannot be saved by performing good works.
- You cannot be saved by avoiding certain major sins.

- You cannot be saved by living better than your neighbor.
- You cannot be saved by joining a church.

Jesus said the only way anyone can be saved is for them to be "born again" (John 3:3). What does that mean? It refers to spiritual rebirth.

The Consequence of Our Sins

Our sins have resulted in our spiritual death. The Bible puts it this way, "The wages of sin is death" (Romans 6:23). We must be spiritually reborn in order to be reconciled to God and have the hope of everlasting life with Him.

How can you experience that spiritual rebirth? By placing your faith in Jesus as your Lord and Savior. That's the only way. Jesus Himself defined salvation as a personal relationship with Him when He said, "This is eternal life, that they may know You, the only true God, and Jesus Christ whom You have sent" (John 17:3).

This vital point makes true Christianity a matter of a relationship, rather than a religion. Religion does not save. Only Jesus saves. Jesus made this crystal clear when He declared, "I am the way, and the truth, and the life; no one comes to the Father but through Me" (John 14:6).

A Forgotten Verse

Everyone seems to know John 3:16, but few seem to be aware of John 3:36. John 3:16 says that "God so loved the world, that He gave His only begotten Son, that whoever believes in Him shall not perish, but have eternal life."John 3:36 says, "He who believes in the Son has eternal life; but he who does not obey the Son will not see life, but the wrath of God abides on him."

This statement in John 3:36, taken from a sermon by John the Baptist, means that everyone alive this moment is under either the grace of God or the wrath of God — one of the two. God *must* deal with sin if He is truly a loving and just God, and He deals with sin in one of two ways — either grace or wrath.

Again, every person on planet earth is under either the grace or the wrath of God. It is a glorious thing to be under God's grace. It is a terrible and tragic thing to be subject to God's wrath.

When Jesus was hanging on the cross, every sin you and I have ever committed and ever will commit was placed upon Him, and He received the wrath of God which you and I deserve. When you accept Jesus as your Lord and Savior, you step into the area where the wrath of God has already fallen, and you become immune to that wrath.

There is a contemporary Christian song that powerfully expresses this truth. It says:[1]

> He paid a debt He did not owe;
> I owed a debt I could not pay;
> I needed someone to wash my sins away.
> And, now, I sing a brand new song,
> "Amazing Grace."
> Christ Jesus paid a debt that I could never pay.

Despite the clear teaching of the Bible that we are saved by grace as a free gift of God, and not by works, there is much confusion in the Christian world about salvation. It would seem that Christendom could give a unified answer to the most important question in the world, "What must I do to be saved?" But unfortunately, that is not the case. You are likely to get as many different answers as the number of Christians you ask.

Salvation by Selection

There are two extreme positions. One extreme, which is the Calvinistic interpretation of predestination, takes the position that God has already predetermined who will be saved and who will be lost. This viewpoint sees Man as so depraved that he is incapable of choosing to follow God. He must be selected by God, and God will select whom He pleases.

The advocates of this viewpoint quote scripture passages like Ephesians 1:4-5: "He chose us in Him before the foundation of the world . . . He predestined us to adoption as sons through Jesus Christ to Himself."

But whom did God choose? Was it specific individuals? The scriptures do not say that. The so-called proof texts for predestination simply establish the fact that God foreordained that those who put their faith in Him would be saved.

The God revealed in the Bible is not a capricious and arbitrary deity who selects a few for salvation and consigns the majority to Hell. He is the God who loved the whole world so much that He sent His only Son to die for the sins of all Mankind (John 3:16).

Salvation by Works

The other extreme viewpoint is known as "works salvation." It argues that people must earn their salvation by performing certain acts to appease the wrath of God. All cultic groups teach works salvation. That's how the Jehovah's Witnesses and the Mormons are able to motivate their people to do door-to-door solicitation.

But many mainline Christian denominations also put an emphasis on works salvation, especially the more conservative, fundamentalist groups. I grew up in such a group, and although we denied a belief in works salvation, we ended up enslaving our people to it by emphasizing a mechanical "plan of salvation."

The essence of salvation, we argued, was a five step plan which many of our preachers referred to as "the five finger exercise." Counting on their fingers, they would name the five steps: "hear, believe, repent, confess and be baptized." We definitely came away from such teaching with the conviction that God was obligated to save any person who performed those five steps in the plan. Some often added a sixth step, namely, a life of faithful obedience to the Lord's commands.

Salvation by Grace

The biblical concept of salvation is not to be found in either of these extremes. Salvation is not conferred arbitrarily by God nor can it be earned by performing certain religious acts.[2]

The Bible approaches the question of salvation by emphasizing that all persons are sinners who are separated from their holy Creator by their sins (Romans 3:9-18). God's Word then makes it clear that no person can justify himself before God through good works. Isaiah says our righteous deeds are like "filthy rags" before the Lord (Isaiah 64:6). Paul affirms that salvation can never be as a "result of works" (Ephesians 2:9).

What hope then do we have? Very much. God has made it possible for us to be reconciled to Him by providing a perfect sacrifice to atone for our sins. God sent His Son, Jesus, to live a perfect life so that He could die, not for His own sins, but for ours. As He hung upon the Cross, the sins of Mankind were placed upon Him, and He received the wrath that we deserved (2 Corinthians 5:21). The blood of Jesus is our only hope (Romans 5:8-9).

The Key Question

This brings us to the central question: How do we appropriate that blood to our lives so that we can receive forgiveness of sins and the hope of eternal life? The Bible's answer is that salvation is a free gift of God's grace which we receive through Jesus by responding to Him in faith (Romans 5:1-2). Here's how Paul puts it in Ephesians 2:8 — "For by grace you have been saved through faith; and that not of yourselves, it is the gift of God."

God's plan of salvation has always been the same — grace through faith. Before the Cross, the focal point of that faith was God the Father and His promise of a Messiah. Since the Cross, the focal point of saving faith has been God the Son, Jesus the Messiah, who died for our sins.

The Faith that Saves

Notice that in the previous sentence I used the term, "saving faith." That term was carefully selected because the faith that saves is something far more substantial than simple belief that Jesus was the Christ, the Son of the living God. After all, the scriptures say that "even the demons believe and tremble" (James 2:19).

Saving faith produces trust in Jesus as one's Savior (John 3:16-17). The faith that saves also produces obedience to God's Word (1 John 5:3). And true saving faith is always manifested in good works (Ephesians 2:10).

The latter point is a paradox. We are not saved by good works. Rather, we are saved to do good works (Titus 2:14). We don't work to be saved. We work because we are saved. True faith will always be manifested in works, "for faith without works is dead" (James 2:14-26).

The Role of Baptism

Where does baptism fit into the picture? The same place as confession and repentance. Saving faith is always demonstrated in repentance, confession and baptism. These are not acts we perform to be saved. Instead, they are obedient responses to God in faith. As a person responds to God in saving faith, he will be compelled by the Holy Spirit to repent of his sins, to confess Jesus as Lord, and to manifest his faith through the symbolic act of baptism.

Baptism is a beautiful symbol of the death, burial and resurrection of Jesus. In like manner, it also symbolizes a death, burial and resurrection that has taken place in the life of the believer — his death to the power and consequence of sin, the burial of his old fleshly self, and his resurrection as a new spiritual being in Christ (Romans 6:3-8).

Some people have dismissed baptism as unimportant and therefore optional. This is a very un-biblical attitude. Jesus commanded baptism (Matthew 28:19). The Apostles baptized all their converts and did so immediately after their confession of faith (Acts 2:38-41, Acts 8:35-38, Acts 10:43-48, and Acts 16:30-33). Peter characterized baptism as "an appeal to God for a good conscience" (I Peter 3:21).

Baptism is always portrayed as a vital step in the initial conversion process. It is the witness that the conversion process has been completed and the discipleship process is ready to begin.

Some people have seized upon baptism as the essence of salvation, and in doing so, they have converted this beautiful, symbolic act into a work to be performed in order to placate God. They argue that "you meet the blood in the water." This is known as "water regeneration."

The baptism that truly saves is not water baptism but the baptism of the Holy Spirit that occurs when one puts his or her faith in Jesus as Lord and Savior. Paul refers to this baptism in 1 Corinthians 12:13 where he says, "By one Spirit we were all baptized into one body."

The Mode of Baptism

The English word, baptism, is a transliteration (not a translation) of the Greek word, *baptizo*. The Greek word means "to immerse." Thus, "John the Baptist" was really John the Immerser.

Immersion as a symbolic rite of purification was well established among the Jews in the time of Jesus. There were many different occasions for such purifications. A woman would immerse herself after her menstrual cycle. Any person who touched a dead body or anything else considered unclean would immerse themselves. This is the reason that nearly all homes of the wealthy contained one or more mikvas — water pools for ceremonial immersions.

Modern excavations have revealed that there were several very large mikvas located at the southern entrance to the Temple Mount in Jerusalem. These were used for ceremonial cleansing before entering the sacred Temple area. And these very pools were probably the ones that Peter and the disciples used on the Day of Pentecost to baptize the 3,000 people who accepted the Gospel (Acts 2:41).

Even scholars from churches that accept other modes of baptism concede that immersion was the only form of baptism practiced by the early church. The alternate techniques of pouring and sprinkling were inventions of men and were never authorized or practiced by the Apostles.

Baptism is a symbol, and symbols are very important. Jesus is called in scripture "the rose of Sharon." He is not referred to as "the tumbleweed of Texas." A biblical symbol is symbolic of a truth, and when we change the symbol, we change the truth it stands for. How can the death, burial and resurrection of the Lord be symbolized in pouring or sprinkling?

The Proper Candidate

Who is a proper candidate for Christian baptism? The first requirement is for the person to hear the Gospel (Romans 10:14). The Gospel is defined in 1 Corinthians 15:1-4 as the death, burial and resurrection of Jesus. The person must then respond to the Gospel with the kind of saving faith (Acts 16:31) that is manifested in repentance (Acts 17:30) and confession (Matthew 10:32).

These qualifications clearly exclude infants as candidates for baptism. The Bible does not contain one example of infant baptism. The only baptism that can be found in the New Testament is the immersion of believing people.

Does that mean that children who die in infancy are lost? Of course not. They are not responsible for their sins since they have not yet reached an age of accountability. On one occasion when children were brought to Jesus, He said, "The kingdom of God belongs to such as these. Truly I say to you, whoever does not receive the kingdom of God like a child shall not enter it at all" (Mark 10:14-15).

Salvation as a Process

There is an interesting point about salvation that is often overlooked. The salvation we immediately experience at the point of faith in Christ is the salvation of our spirit. The Holy Spirit regenerates our spirit which is dead in sin. The Bible refers to this as justification (Galatians 2:16).

But that is not the end of salvation, and that is the reason that the Bible speaks of salvation as an ongoing process (I Corinthians 1:18). The salvation of the soul (the mind, emotions and personality) begins at the point of faith, but it continues throughout one's lifetime. This process is called sanctification (Romans 6:18-19).

The change agent, once again, is the Holy Spirit. When a person is born again through the regeneration of his spirit, the Holy Spirit takes up residence inside the person and begins to shape his soul into the image of Jesus (Romans 8:29-30, 2 Corinthians 3:18, and Galatians 4:19).

Our salvation will not be completed until the resurrection of the righteous. At that time, our bodies will be saved as God miraculously reconstitutes them and then glorifies them, making them immortal and perfect (Romans 8:18-23 and 1 Corinthians 15:50-57).

Thus, our salvation is past, present and future — justification (the spirit), sanctification (the soul), and glorification (the body).

The True Meaning of Salvation

This brings us back to the essence of salvation. I want to emphasize once again that it is a relationship with a Man and not obedience to a plan. We become saved by putting our trust in a person, and we remain saved by continuing to trust in that person.

That person, of course, is Jesus of Nazareth who was God in the flesh (John 1:1-14). That is why Jesus said, "I am the way, and the truth, and the life; no one comes to the Father, but through Me" (John 14:6). It is also the reason that Jesus said, "This is eternal life, that they know You, the only true God, and Jesus Christ whom You have sent" (John 17:3).

The essence of Christianity is a relationship with a person. You enter that relationship by an act of faith whereby you accept Jesus as your Lord and Savior.

> "Without faith it is impossible to please God, for he who comes to God must believe that He is, and that He is a rewarder of those who seek Him" (Hebrews 11:6).

If you have never put your faith in Jesus as your Lord and Savior, I invite you to do so now. Confess to God that you are a sinner and ask Him to forgive you of your sins. And then receive Jesus as your Savior. Once you have done this, seek out a Bible believing church where Jesus is exalted as the only hope for the world. Go before that church and confess your faith and then manifest that faith in water baptism. Then, seek out a Bible study and prayer group within that church where you can begin to grow in your faith.

Having done this, you will be ready for the return of the Lord, and you can join with me and many other Christians who welcome each day with great hope by exclaiming, "Maranatha! Come quickly, Lord Jesus." ✜

Believers Win In The End!

"When the thousand years [of Jesus' reign on earth] are completed, Satan will be released from his prison, and will come out to deceive the nations which are in the four corners of the earth, Gog and Magog, to gather them together for the war; the number of them is like the sand of the seashore. And they came up on the broad plain of the earth and surrounded the camp of the saints and the beloved city, and fire came down from heaven and devoured them. And the devil who deceived them was thrown into the lake of fire and brimstone, where the beast [the Antichrist] and the false prophet are also; and they will be tormented day and night forever and ever." — Revelation 20:7-10

REFERENCES

Part 1:
The Antichrist in Scripture

A Time of Unparalleled Horror

Several books are recommended for further study regarding the Great Tribulation:

Chuck Smith, *The Great Tribulation and the Church* (Costa Mesa, CA: Word for Today, 1980).

John Walvoord, *The Blessed Hope and the Tribulation* (Grand Rapids, MI: Zondervan, 1977).

Thomas Ice and Kenneth L. Gentry, *The Great Tribulation: Past or Future?* (Grand Rapids, MI: Kregel Academic, 1999).

The *Left Behind* series of 16 novels by Tim LaHaye and Jerry Jenkins are based on the story of the Tribulation as contained in the book of Revelation. This series was published by Tyndale House (1995-2007).

A Tyrant of Unbridled Ruthlessness

Responsible books recommended for a further study of the Antichrist include the following:

Arthur W. Pink, *The Antichrist: A Study of Satan's Christ* (Redford, VA: Wilder Publications, 2009). This is a reprint of the original book that was published in 1923. The complete text is available on the Internet at www.biblebelievers.com/Pink/anti christ01.htm.

Ed Hindson, *Antichrist Rising: The Coming Global Storm* (Springfield, MO: 21st Century Press, 2003), 240 pages.

Mark Hitchcock, *Who is the Antichrist? Answering the Question Everyone is Asking* (Eugene, OR: Harvest House Publishers, 2011), 198 pages.

Ron Rhodes, *Unmasking the Antichrist: Dispelling the Myths, Discerning the Truth* (Eugene, OR: Harvest House Publishers, 2012), 256 pages.

Part 2:
A Prophetic Forum About the Antichrist

Introduction to the Forum

1) All the Bible prophecy experts featured in this forum approach the study of prophecy from a literal or plain sense viewpoint. They are all Premillennial and Pre-Tribulational, meaning that they believe the Rapture of the Church will take place before the onset of the Great Tribulation and that the Tribulation will be ended with the return of Jesus to earth to reign for a thousand years from Jerusalem.

2) Stephen J. Nichols, "Prophecy Makes Strange Bedfellows: On the History of Identifying the Antichrist," *Journal of the Evangelical Theological Society*, 44:1 (March 2001), pages 87-105, www.theologicalstudies.org.uk/article_esch_nichols.html, page 5.

3) Nichols, page 6.

4) Ibid.

5) Ibid., page 7.

Part 3:
An In-Depth Look at Four Issues

The Persistent Wars of the End Times

1) Joel Rosenberg, *Epicenter: Why the Current Rumbling in the Middle East Will Change Your Future* (Carol Stream, IL: Tyndale House Publishers, 2006), 312 pages.

2) Bill Salus, *Isralestine: The Ancient Blueprints of the Future Middle East* (Lecompton , KS: High Way Publishing, 2008), 350 pages.

3) Ron Rhodes, *Northern Storm Rising: Russia, Iran, and the Emerging End-Times Military Coalition Against Israel* (Eugene, OR: Harvest House Publishers, 2008), 256 pages.

The Location of the Antichrist's Headquarters

1) Most of those who are currently proposing sites in the United States are conspiracy theorists. For some good examples, see:

   a) The Omega Days, "New York City: The Throne of the Antichrist," www.theomegadays.net/ topics/tyre.htm.

   b) End Timez, "The United Nations," www.endtimez.com/united nations.html.

   c) The Cutting Edge, "Masonic Symbols of Power in Their Seat of Power — Washington, D.C.," www.cuttingedge.org/n1040.html.

2) Charles Dyer, *The Rise of Babylon* (Carol Stream, IL: Tyndale House, 1991).

3) Information about The World Monuments Fund can be found on the Internet at www.wmf.org.

The Possibility of a Muslim Antichrist

1) Joel Richardson, *Antichrist: Islam's Awaited Messiah*, (Enumclaw, WA: WinePress Publishing, 2006), 276 pages.

2) Joel Richardson, *The Islamic Antichrist: The Shocking Truth About the Real Nature of the Beast*, (Los Angeles, CA: WND Books, 2009), 271 pages.

3) Walid Shoebat, *God's War on Terror: Islam, Prophecy and the Bible*, (Lafayette, LA: Top Executive Media, 2008), 512 pages.

4) Walid Shoebat, *Why I Left Jihad,* (Lafayette, LA: Top Executive Media, 2005), 412 pages. Shoebat's claim to have been a former Palestinian terrorist has been hotly disputed in several articles that can be found on the Internet.

5) Wikipedia, "Sahih al-Bukhari," http://en.wikipedia.org/wiki/Sahih_al-Bukhari#Number_of_hadith.

6) Samuel Shahid, *The Last Trumpet: A Comparative Study in Christian-Islamic Eschatology*, (Longwood, FL: Xulon Press, 2005), 305 pages.

7) Shahid, page 28.

8) Ibid., pages 30-33. See also: G. F. Haddad, "Signs of the Hour," www.livingislam.org/n/signh_e.html.

9) Ibid., pages 34-42.

10) Mission Islam, "Who is the Evil Dajjal ?" www.missionislam.com/nwo/whoisdajjal.htm. See also, Shahid, pages 45-47.

11) Idara Dawat-o-Irshad, USA, Inc., "Identification of the Prophesied Imam Mahdi," www.irshad.org/islam/ prophecy/mahdi.htm.. See also Richardson, *Antichrist*, pages 40-51.

12) Mufti A.H. Elias, "Jesus (Isa) in Islam, and his Second Coming," www.islam.tc/prophecies/jesus.html. See also, Shahid, pages 73-89.

13) Elias, "Jesus in Islam . . ." See also, Shahid, pages 111-113.

14) Wikipedia, "Islamic Eschatology," http://en.wikipedia.org/wiki/Islamic_ eschatology. See also, Shahid, pages 167-191.

15) HilalPlaza, "The Day of Judgment," www.hilalplaza.com/islam/day-of-judgment.html. See also, Shahid, pages 192-210.

16) Richardson, *Antichrist*, pages 50-51 and 78-79.

17) Ibid., pages 80, 94, and 187.

18) Ibid., pages 67-68.

19) Ibid., pages 136-154.

20) Ibid., pages 66-67.

21) Ibid., pages 110-114.

22) Shahid, Pages 45-72. See also, Wikipedia, "Masih ad-Dajjal," http://en.wikipedia.org/wiki/Masih_ad-Dajjal.

23) HNN Staff (History News Network), "What Is the Difference Between Sunni and Shiite Muslims – and Why Does It Matter?" http://hnn.us/articles/934.html.

24) Wikipedia, "The Occultation," http://en.wikipedia.org/wiki/The_Occultation.

25) HNN Staff, "What is the Difference . . ."

26) Jacob Prasch, "The Islamic Antichrist: the Unresolved Problems with Joel Richardson's Theory," September 11, 2009, www.moriel.org/MorielArchive/index.php/news/uk/the-islamic-antichrist.

27) Prasch, "The Islamic Antichrist . . .", page 3.

28) Ibid., page 3.

29) Richardson, *Antichrist*, page 215.

30) Ibid., page 216.

31) Wikiquote, "Voltaire," http://en.wikiquote.org/wiki/Voltaire.

32) Richardson, *Antichrist*, pages 103-104.

33) Ron Rhodes, *Northern Storm Rising* (Eugene, OR: Harvest House, 2008), pages 104-109. See also: Mark Hitchcock, *The Coming Islamic Invasion of Israel* (Sisters, OR: Multnomah, 2002), pages 31-32.

34) Ron Rhodes, *Northern Storm Rising*, pages 102-104.

35) Richardson, *Antichrist,* page 109.

36) Ibid., pages 121-128.

37) Ibid., pages 197-202.

38) Ibid., pages 203-204.

39) Bill Salus has written an excellent book on the prophetic implications of Psalm 83. It is titled, *Isralestine*, (Lecompton, KS: High Way Publishers, 2008), 350 pages.

40) Shoebat, *God's War on Terror*, pages 197-198.

41) Ibid., pages 267-274.

42) Ibid., pages 240-243.

43) Ibid., page 241.

44) Ibid., pages 349-353.

45) Ibid., pages 369-371.

46) Ibid., page 371.

47) Joel Richardson, "Daniel 9:26: Who Are the People of the Prince to Come?" www.joelstrumpet.com/?p=2440.

48) Ibid., pages 3-4.

49) Joel Richardson, "EU Collapse: Doom for Popular Bible Prophesies?" www.wnd.com/index.php?fa=PAGE.view&pageId=160393.

50) Quote supplied by Lambert Dolphin (http://ldolphin.org).

The Naming of the Antichrist

1) Joe Kovacs, "Did Jesus actually reveal the name of the Antichrist?" WorldNetDaily, www.wnd.com/?pageID=105527.

2) Wikipedia, "Gematria," http://en.wikipedia.org/wiki/Gematria.

3) Mark Hitchcock, "A Critique of the Preterist View of Revelation 13 and Nero," *Bibliotheca Sacra*, 164 (July-September 2007), pp. 341-356.

4) Gary Bowers, *Out of the Abyss* (Bloomington, IN: WestBow Press, 2011), 286 pages.

5) Bowers, pp. 189-201.

6) John Claeys, *Apocalypse 2012: The Ticking of the End Time Clock* (Sister, OR: VMI Publishers, 2010), 275 pages.

7) For a defense of the 95 AD date of the book of Revelation, see, "The Date of Revelation" by Thomas Ice, www.pre-trib.org/data/pdf/Ice-TheDateoftheBookof Re.pdf.

8) Claeys, p. 183.

9) Ibid., p. 149.

10) Tim Cohen, *The Antichrist and a Cup of Tea* (Aurora, CO: Prophecy House, 1998), 444 pages.

11) Cohen, p. 9. In 1995 Monte Judah began to teach that the Tribulation began in September 1993 when the Arab-Israeli Peace Agreement was signed. He prophesied that the altar of the Jewish Temple would be rebuilt, sacrifices would begin, and the sacrifices would be stopped by February or March of 1997. He even went so far as to say that if he was proved wrong, "I will be guilty of misleading God's people." And he added that if he was wrong, it would be clear that "God did not call me to be a prophet."

12) Ibid., p. 58.

13) Ibid., p. 60.

14) Joe VanKoevering, *Unveiling the Man of Sin* (St. Petersburg, FL: God's News Publishing, 2007),

15) VanKoevering, p. 78.

16) Ibid., p. 93.

17) Early Christian Writings, "Irenaeus of Lyons," www.earlychris tianwritings.com/irenaeus.html.

The God of the Antichrist

1) The Barna Group, "Most American Christians Do Not Believe that Satan or the Holy Spirit Exist," www.barna.org. Also, see Religious Tolerance, "About Ghosts, Satan, Heaven, Hell, etc.," www.religioustolerance.org.
2) Religious Tolerance, "About Ghosts, Satan . . ."
3) Conan O'Brien, "I'm Gonna Go to Hell When I Die!" www.jesus-is-savior.com.
4) Sam Lavender, "God Made A Way," www.voiceoftheevangelists.com.
5) AC/DC, "Highway to Hell," www.lyricsfreak.com.
6) Acheron, "The Rites of the Black Mass," www.av1611.org.
7) Metallica, "The Prince," www.sing365.com.
8) Wes Penre, "Satanic Quotes by Musicians," www.illuminati-news.com.

Part 4:
Good News For Christians

The Escape of the Church

1) Early Christian Writings, "Justin Martyr," www.earlychristianwritings.com/justin.html.
2) Paul Boyer, *When Time Shall Be No More: Prophecy Belief in Modern American Culture* (Cambridge, MA: Belknap Press, 1992), page 75.
3) C. I. Scofield, *The Scofield Study Bible* (London: Oxford University Press, 1909).
4) Paul N. Benware, *Understanding End Times Prophecy: A Comprehensive Approach* (Chicago: Moody Press, 1995), pages 197-198.

The Timing of the Escape

1) Early Christian Writings, "The Shepherd of Hermas," 2[23]:5, www.earlychristianwritings.com/shepherd.html.
2) Timothy J. Denny and Thomas D. Ice, "The Rapture and an Early Medieval Citation," *Bibliotheca Sacra*, July-September 1995,

pages 306-317.

3) The Catholic Encyclopedia, "St. Ephraem," www.newadvent.org/cathen/05498a.htm.

4) Tommy Ice, "Morgan Edwards: A Pre-Darby Rapturist," The Conservative Theological Journal, April 1997, pages 4-12.

5) Tim LaHaye, "Target Number One," Pre-Trib Perspectives, September 2002, pages 1-3.

6) William E. Blackstone, *Jesus is Coming* (1878). The modern day version is published by Kregel (1989).

7) C. I. Scofield, *The Scofield Study Bible* (London: Oxford University Press, 1909).

8) Clarence Larkin, *Dispensational Truth* (Philadelphia, 1918), 176 pages.

9) Ed Reese, "Henry (Harry) Allan Ironside," booklet in the Christian Hall of Fame series (Lansing, IL: Reese Publications), www.eaec.org/faithhallfame/harryironside.htm.

10) Hal Lindsey with C. C. Carlson, *The Late Great Planet Earth* (Grand Rapids, MI: Zondervan, 1970), 192 pages.

11) Beginning in 1996 Tim LaHaye and Jerry Jenkins started publishing a series of scriptural novels about the Rapture which came to be known as "The Left Behind" books. A total of 12 volumes have been published in the series, and to date, they have sold 65 million copies.

12) Dave MacPherson, *The Unbelievable Pre-Trib Origin* (Heart of America Bible Society, 1973), 123 pages. The author has republished this book over the years under several different titles. For an excellent commentary on MacPherson's theory, see "Dave MacPherson: Inventor of False Pre-Trib History" by Tommy Ice, http://raptureready.com/ who/Dave_MacPherson.html.

13) Dave MacPherson, *The Incredible Cover-Up: Exposing the Origins of the Rapture Theories* (Plainfield, NJ: Logos 1975) page 85.

14) MacPherson, pages 151-154.

Part 5:
Are You Ready?

Epilogue

1) Ellis J. Crum, "He Paid A Debt He Did Not Owe," www.touchjesussongs.net/lyricspage15.html.

2) For a detailed discussion of all aspects of salvation, consult the book, *Eternity: Heaven or Hell?* by David R. Reagan (McKinney, TX: Lamb & Lion Ministries, 2010), 195 pages.

Dr. Reagan's Comprehensive Book About Bible Prophecy

What is the destiny of planet earth?

What is going to be the fate of mankind?

We don't have to guess. The Bible spells out God's plan for the ages in great detail through prophecies given thousands of years ago.

In this book Dr. Reagan presents a panoramic survey of the fundamentals of Bible prophecy, with a focus on the prophecies that relate to the end times. In the process, he reveals God's plan for the redemption of mankind and the restoration of the creation.

The book is written in a down-to-earth, easy-to-understand style. Although all the chapters relate to the overall theme, each chapter is designed to stand alone. This makes it possible for you either to read the book straight through or to skip around, reading only those chapters whose topics appeal to you.

The book is divided into five parts:

Prophetic Significance
Prophetic Issues
Prophetic Viewpoints
Prophetic Signs
Prophetic Hope

There is a Prophetic Epilogue in which Dr. Reagan presents an in-depth, verse by verse explanation of Psalm 2, one of the Bible's greatest passages about the Second Coming of the Lord.

The book contains 42 chapters and runs 415 pages in length. It sells for $15. You can order a copy by calling 800-705-8316, Monday through Friday, 8am to 5pm Central time. You can also purchase the book through the Lamb & Lion website at www.lamblion.com.

Dr. Reagan's Video Overview of Bible Prophecy

This album contains six programs on two DVDs. Each program runs about 25 minutes in length, for a total of 150 minutes. The album loads with a menu that enables the viewer to jump immediately to any one of the six programs.

All six lessons were presented by Dr. David Reagan before live audiences. They provide a comprehensive introduction to all the fundamentals of Bible prophecy:

- The Abuse of Bible Prophecy
- The Importance of Bible Prophecy
- The Variety of Bible Prophecy
- The Interpretation of Bible Prophecy
- The End Time Viewpoints
- The Signs of the Times

One of the DVD discs contains printable files for a Teacher's Manual and Student Study Guides.

This album is a great resource for both learning and teaching Bible prophecy. Each presentation is lavishly illustrated with pictures, charts, and diagrams. The album sells for $25.

You can order a copy by calling 800-705-8316, Monday through Friday, 8am to 5pm Central time. You can also purchase the book through the Lamb & Lion website at www.lamblion.com.

The Lamb & Lion Website

The Lamb & Lion website is an interactive site that you can use to pose questions to the ministry's Web Minister. The site also contains a host of articles about every aspect of Bible prophecy. Additionally, you can view the ministry's television programs on the site and read copies of the ministry's magazine. The ministry's catalogue of Bible prophecy resources can also be found on the website, and orders can be placed from the site.